Ed

D0946638

Jim Zabel

I LOVE IT
I LOVE IT
I LOVE IT

65 Years of Fun and Games

With Rich Wolfe

© Rich Wolfe

Published by Lone Wolfe Press, a division of Richcraft. Distribution, marketing, publicity, interviews, and book signings handled by Wolfegang Marketing Systems, Ltd.—But Not Very.

Selected photographs reprinted with permission. This book is not affiliated with or endorsed by the University of Iowa or the NCAA.

No part of this book may be reproduced, stored in a retrieval system, or transmitted, in any form or by any means, electronic, mechanical, photocopying, recording, or otherwise, without the prior permission of Rich Wolfe.

Rich Wolfe can be reached at 602-738-5889
Layout: The Printed Page, Phoenix, AZ
Author's agent: T. Roy Gaul

ISBN: 978-0-9800978-9-4

DEDICATION

This book is dedicated to the fans who provided the audience through the years, to the management that provided the opportunity, to the athletes who provided the inspiration, and to my wife, Jill, whose diligence and devotion have sustained me and, in fact, have been the driving forces behind this literary effort. To one and all, my deepest all-inclusive thanks.

ACKNOWLEDGMENTS

For their help in providing artwork, photos, printed material and other artistic assistance, I wish to thank *The Des Moines Register* and columnist, Sean Keeler (Foreword), especially for permission to include several photos from the "Hawkeye for Eternity" article by Ken Fuson (© 1994) on pages 44, 51, 56, 82, 106, 164, 125, and 234. In addition, the cover photos are also used with permission of *The Des Moines Register*. Thanks also to the *Quad-City Times*, the *Arizona Republic*, the *Cedar Rapids Gazette*, and *The Daily Iowan* newspapers; *The Iowan* magazine and *Iowa History Journal*; the Sports Information departments, University of the University of Iowa and Drake University; *Cyclone Illustrated*; Joel McCrea and Steve Parrott (WHO Archives); Mike Finn (Iowa Football Vault); and Chuck Offenburger, Mike Chapman, Sue Reichardt, Bill Logan, Mike Mahon, Phil Haddy and others who donated private materials. Sincere thanks to all, and special votes of appreciation to publishing masterminds Rich Wolfe and Lisa Liddy, and to those who planted the seeds of the idea for this book and encouraged its growth—Sean Keeler, Steve Parrott, Ed Podolak, Joel McCrea, and Jill Zabel.

FOREWORD

What's he like? He makes an hour feel like 15 minutes. He is a breeze and a song. He is Peter Pan and the Pied Piper, forever young, beckoning us to follow down the roads of our dreams.

Jim Zabel has entertained presidents, chased icons and crowned kings. He traveled the world, then turned it into his oyster. Hell, even if only half his stories are true, that's twice as much adventure in one lifetime as the rest of us figure to get. If we're lucky.

And yet, deep down, beneath the hyperbole and the microphones, Jim is a man true to his roots. He never stopped being a child of the Depression. His penuriousness has taken on a life of its own — compared to Z, Wimpy from those old "Popeye" comic strips looks like Thurston Howell — but it's also rooted in genuine conviction, the verities of youth.

"So the first time we went on a trip," recalls Jim Walden, the former Iowa State football coach and Z's old partner on Iowa Barnstormers radio broadcasts. "I look up and Jim Zabel, he's got a little bag of cheese sticks and some little sausages. He's opening the can and having dinner. And I said, 'What is this, are we back to the Oklahoma Gold Rush or what?'

"How much money does this man spend, that he's sitting there, he's got some crackers, a stick of cheese, some Vienna Sausages, and he's eating it just like it was steak and eggs, man! I thought, 'Either he's cheaper than I thought he was, or his mother probably told him to always pack a lunch.' And he was saving money at the same time."

What's he like? He's a Vienna Sausage guy with caviar pipes, blessed with a quick wit and a mind like a bear trap. He poured his guts into his beloved Hawkeyes, in good times and bad, then dragged your heartstrings along for the ride.

For hundreds of thousands of people, across generations, he was the soundtrack of a state. A friend to slap us on the back and guide us through brisk football autumns, brutal basketball winters, soggy Drake Relays springs, and sweltering State Fair summers. A signpost from planting to harvest, and all the roller-coaster rides in between.

What's he like? Lord, he's fun. Straight as an arrow, blunt as a truncheon. He can be politically incorrect, but never out of spite or malice. He likes good friends and a cold beverage at the end of a hard day, and makes no apologies for it. Buy him a round, he'll spin yarns into a cardigan. A pinch of Hemingway, a dash of Jacob Grimm.

Like my father before me, I grew up listening to Z call games on the radio, his voice painting pictures on the easel of my mind. I must've bumped into him a dozen times over the last decade, either in the WHO studio or at Drake Stadium. At each and every meeting, he'd never fail to a.) thank me for the column I wrote about him a few years ago; and b.) rave about how much he liked a story I wrote that had nothing to do with sports at all — a piece about a rainy afternoon in Norfolk, Neb., the aftermath of a chilling bank murder.

What's he like? He is a pillar and a mentor, a walking Wikipedia, the fount of founts. If you can't find something to talk to Z about, you're not trying. When he discovered I was a fan of classic films, we spent the next 25 minutes — two grown men, born more than 50 years apart — gushing about the glory that is the Turner Classic Movies cable network. He knew I loved football history, especially Big Ten football history; I'd constantly try to pick his brain during commercial breaks. He'd be rolling through another of his 1,001 anecdotes and before long, we'd both be laughing so hard the chairs would shake.

What's he like? He's infectious. Infectious and real. Talk to Dick Vitale or Lee Corso or Bob Knight once the cameras are turned off, and it's as if they're a completely different person, an actor who's stepped off stage and removed his mask. Not Z. When he tells you to hug and kiss your radios, every word comes straight from deep within the soul.

Jim didn't just talk at you; he talked with you. In that sense, he was ahead of his time, a harbinger of the interactive train that now drives 21st century media. At the start of Z's journey, folks got their information from newspapers and radio. Today, they read headlines on their cellular phones, fast forward through commercial breaks with their digital recorders, and use message boards to vent their frustrations to the masses. Columnists became bloggers, and vice versa. Penn State pulled off the unthinkable by joining the Big Ten. Nebraska pulled off something even more unthinkable by doing the same. Borders were redrawn. The money train rolled ever onward. Jim Zabel is Jim Zabel, forever and always.

And now he's written it all down. Finally. I love it, I love it, I love it.

Sean Keeler
Sports columnist
The Des Moines Register

TABLE CONTENTS

JUST THE STATS...

Full Name: James Frederick Zabel

Born: Sept. 3, 1921, Davenport, Iowa

Birth Weight: 10.6 pounds...
Weight Today: 175 pounds Height 6-1 ½

Parents: Fred W. & Verna E. Zabel

Sister: Joan E. Humm, Scottsdale, AZ

Children: Jane E. Paul, born 1952—Spouse: Jeff Paul
Diane M. Webster, born 1960, (Deceased 2009)

Step-children: Jennifer Williams, born 1974, Jeff Williams, born 1979

Grandchildren: Annie Paul Gibson, Minneapolis, A.J. Paul, Charlie Paul, Davenport

Great Grandchild: Christopher Gibson, Minneapolis

Former wife: Mary Janice Boehm—Married 1946 (Deceased 1985)

Wife: Jill H. Williams—Married 1997, Scottsdale, AZ

Education: Pierce Grade School, Sudlow Middle School, Davenport High School, University of Iowa, B.A. Degree 1944; Major: Journalism Minor: English

Date of employment at WHO: May 18, 1944

Sports broadcast history: 6,000 play-by-play events, including every Iowa football and basketball game for 50 years, five Rose Bowl Games, three Holiday Bowls, two Peach Bowls, two Alamo Bowls, two Sun Bowls, Gator Bowl, Freedom Bowl, Kickoff Classic (New York), 48 NCAA Basketball Tournament Games, 10 NIT Tournament Games, Iowa High School Boys

and Girls Basketball Tournaments for 52 years, selected bas-
ketball games of Drake and Iowa State for 20 years, Drake
Relays for 60 years, "Let's Go Bowling" (WHO-TV) for 33 years,
eleven Iowa Triple-A Baseball games on WHO-TV, 10 Shrine
All-Star Football Games, seven years of Iowa Barnstormers
Arena Football on WHO Radio (approximately 150 games).
Five major golf tournaments on WHO-TV, including National
Amateur in 1956, at Wakonda Club.

Honors: Marconi Award (Personality of the Year, 1993) from
National Association of Broadcasters; Des Moines Register
Hall of Fame (2007); Iowa Broadcasters Hall of Fame; Des
Moines Sports Hall of Fame; Iowa Sportscaster of the Year;
I-Club Man of the Year (twice); Polk County I-Club Man of the
Year; Variety Club "Sportsman of the Year"; Grand Marshall of
the Iowa Homecoming Parade and honored guest at Home-
coming Game (twice, 1992 and 2003); Iowa Press Box "Wall of
Fame"; Southeast Iowa I-Club "Man of the Year" (Ottumwa);
Iowa Letterman's Ring (honorary); Distinguished Service
Awards from Iowa High School Athletic Association; Iowa Girls
Union, Drake Relays and Iowa State Bowling Proprietors Asso-
ciation; "Golden Voices of Football" two entries, Iowa v. Notre
Dame—1953, and Iowa v. Ohio State—1987, "Jim Zabel Day"
in Davenport, May 15, 2004, proclaimed by Mayor Charles W.
Brooke.

Likes & Dislikes: Favorite things about Iowa—Tomatoes,
sweet corn and October, and of course the Iowa Hawkeyes and
their wonderful fans. Believe me, there are no greater people
than those in Iowa. Unfavorite thing about Iowa—the weather
in winter. (I remember the TV shot last winter of the guy with
a snow-blower standing on his roof)

Favorite meal: Corned beef and cabbage (prepared by Jill)

Favorite singer: Sinatra, of course. Was there anyone else?
(I saw him 26 times). Oh, yes, and Elvis!

Chapter 1

DEEP ROOTS

Big Dreams

DAVENPORT!

If Oklahoma! warrants an exclamation point, why not Davenport? After all, it was the first city in Iowa, the gateway to the early west, the birthplace of jazz great Bix Beiderbecke, and the home of the oldest high school west of the Mississippi River. That's right—Davenport High celebrated its' 150th anniversary several years ago, and I did a piece for the Quad City Times talking about my fond memories of my days at DHS.

Davenport was a great place to grow up. It was the most social town I have ever seen. (It still is today. When I last checked, my contemporaries had established a new ritual—"the Monday night cocktail party," the thought being that the normal weekend festivities were not enough. They needed to be expanded. Oh, well, as Humphrey Bogart once said, "One martini is too many, and ten aren't enough.")

We had high school fraternities and sororities in my day. There were dances and "hops" every weekend, and during the Christmas holidays we had dances almost every night and tea dances many afternoons, a lot of them formal. I have often said I wore my tux and tails more at Davenport High School than I have ever since. In fact, I don't know where they are now and I am sure they would not fit.

Some of our favorite hangouts included Zoom Inn, by the Davenport Airport, the Honey Malted Shop in Rock Island and the Rendezvous Club in Moline, featuring the Speck Redd Band. We danced at the Coliseum Ballroom, where the big bands played, the Moline Elks, the Outing Club and the Blackhawk Hotel.

When we took our dates out for an evening of fine dining, we went to the Plantation in Moline, a stately old mansion renowned for its cuisine. I came across an old menu from the Plantation and was astounded by some of those Depression Day prices. How about a lobster cocktail for 85 cents, a whole broiled Maine lobster for $3.50, a charcoal broiled New York sirloin steak for $3.50 and a large porterhouse for two for $7.00. (Eat your heart out).

Memories of Davenport High School track

Life in Davenport those days revolved around the high school. We were the largest school in the state and we had great athletic programs. DHS won more than 120 state championships over the years, and I must admit I am proud to be a part of that legacy. I captained the Blue Devils track team my senior year. We won the state indoor track championship, and I will never forget what happened when I presented the trophy to our principal at an auditorium assembly the next Monday. There was no place to put it. The trophy cases were all full. Finally, they found space for it on a table in the basement.

We finished second in the state outdoor meet that year. Davenport and Des Moines East were tied at 33 points going into the final event, the mile relay, which I anchored for the Blue Devils. The great Frank Kaiser (who later set a national 400 meter AAU record) anchored for East. He beat me to the tape by about half a step in the sensational time (for that day) of 48.3 seconds. Years later, when I was announcing the auto races at the fairgrounds, I ran into Frank. He was a police officer. We reminisced about the old days, then as we parted, Frank said, "Don't try anything funny. Remember, I can still catch you."

One athletic experience I will never forget took place in June of my senior year. My coach, Jesse Day, called and said he wanted me to run an exhibition race before a baseball game at Douglas Ball Park in Rock Island the next night. I was kind of a cocky kid, so I said "Who will I run against? I've already beaten everyone in this area." My coach said "you haven't beaten this guy. It's Jesse Owens." Oh, my God, I thought! My hero! Jesse Owens!

He held every world record from the 50-yard dash through the 220-yard dash, the low hurdles and the broad jump. So, I appeared at the Douglas Ball Park the next night in my Blue Devil track outfit. Owens was in his Olympic uniform. How did I do? Well, like I tell people once the race started, I never saw his face. He ran a 9.8 that night. I came in a little bit later.

Owens became a friend. I had him on my show many times through the years. (I covered his funeral for NBC when he passed away in Phoenix. His body lay in state at the Arizona Statehouse).

I hit another track milestone when the Mississippi Valley Fair invited me to run an exhibition 100-yard dash against a horse and a Model-T in front of the grandstand. I beat the Model-T, but I'll swear the horse thought it was the Kentucky Derby. Man, could he move.

Apparently, my track exploits must have impressed somebody. The University of Iowa offered me a full scholarship; coach George Bresnahan met with me personally. I also got a scholarship offer from Kirksville College in Missouri, and letters of inquiry from Northwestern and Purdue. I will have to admit I had Olympic dreams as a 17-year-old, but reality set in after I ran against Owens.

What kind of a kid was I in Davenport? I had a lot of energy, and sometimes it got me in trouble. I wasn't really bad. I was just adventuresome. One time I stole a steamroller, (that was back in the days when steamrollers were really run by steam). A city crew was paving Forest Road, and they left a steamroller with a full head of steam. My friend Jim Bechtel and I could not resist the temptation. We took the huge machine for a little drive. Finally, some cooler heads appeared on the scene and told us to take the steamroller back where we found it. So, I put it in reverse and moved it back where we started, about a block up the street. We received some pretty stiff reprimands from our parents. But I'll have to admit a steamroller ride is something special.

I had a number of summer jobs during those early days in Davenport, mainly mowing lawns, delivering newspapers and caddying. Finally, when I was 16, I landed a job ushering at the Capitol Theater. These were Depression Days. I made 25 cents an hour, plus all the free movies I could watch. My boss was "Beefy" Gillon. (In a strange quirk of fate, his son Matt was one of my bosses at WHO).

One of the highlights of the week was "Bank Night," and the highlight for me was that I was selected to turn the drum on stage and then pick the winner of the big prize, usually $500. The emcee for Bank Night was Dutch Reagan's brother, Moon Reagan, who was an announcer on WOC and did "Man on the Street" shows. The toughest part of the evening came earlier. Theater admissions in those days were 25 cents. But Bank Night posed a problem. Under Iowa law, you could not charge an entry fee to take part in a game of chance. That meant that people theoretically could get free admissions simply by asking for them. To counter this free give away possibility, our District Manager, Joe Kinskey, coached us on how to embarrass patrons into buying tickets. "You say to them, "What's the matter, are you too cheap to buy a ticket?" Kinskey said, "Insult them. Make them feel bad." I hated this part of the job, but I loved being on stage with Moon Reagan. (Incidentally, Moon went on to Hollywood after Dutch did, and became vice president of McCann Erickson Advertising. I had lunch with him when I was covering the Rose Bowl in 1958. We met at an upscale restaurant in Hollywood. I'll never forget what he said when we sat down. "I hope your day went better than mine. I spent the morning with Frank Sinatra. Chesterfield is doing a new TV show with him, and he drives a hard bargain.")

I was a favorite of Joe Kinskey, I think. He called me into his office and asked me to pick up his wife at the Rock Island train depot. "She's coming in from Chicago on the 8 o'clock Rocket," Kinskey said. "Be sure to wear your uniform".

Not exactly Fred Astaire but I did have the white tie and tails and Davenport was a social place.

So, there I was, driving Joe's big Buick Roadmaster, and opening the car door for Mrs. Kinskey. Obviously Joe wanted everyone to think he had a chauffeur. And for one night, he did.

My theater days lasted until I got out of high school. I was 17, and I had wanderlust. I wanted to see the world. (The reason why I was so young is that you had to be 5 by September 4 to enter kindergarten, and my birthday is Sept. 3.) I knew I wanted to go to college, but figured I could wait a year. I had adventure in my heart, I was restless. Richard Halliburton was the big travel lecturer of the day. I read all of his books and saw his lecture at Davenport High School. He talked about swimming the Panama Canal and crossing the Alps like Hannibal did. I was entranced. I had a friend named Kibby who felt the same way I did. He wanted to travel. (Kibby was state AAU heavyweight wrestling champion, and I was quarter mile track champ. So, between the two of us, I thought we could out-fight or out-run trouble).

Kibby and I frankly had more guts than sense. We thought we would hitchhike to New Orleans, and then work our way to Rio de Janeiro on a tramp steamer. My dear mother thought I had seen too many Errol Flynn movies, but went along with my "fantasizing", thinking that it was a temporary thing. In fact, she even offered to drive us to the edge of town. So shortly after July 4th we started out, two intrepid travelers in search of adventure.

As I look back on that whole thing, it is one part of my own life I can hardly believe. Was I crazy? No, we were just young, full of get up and go, and the belief that the sky was the limit.

Remember, this was not today. This was a time when hitchhiking was safer and people helped each other. We made it to St. Louis on the first day, and slept in a hay stack. We went to Memphis and then to New Orleans, sleeping on benches and in an abandoned filling station. Our tramp steamer idea turned out to be a pipe dream. You had to have a Seaman's card to get on a tramp steamer, and we didn't have the experience. Then it was over to San Antonio, riding a freight train part of the way, and that night we climbed the wall of the Alamo and slept on the soft grass until we were kicked out in the morning. True story. After that we went to Nuevo Laredo, just across the border and caught the bus to Mexico City. (Hitchhiking in Mexico? Nada).

Mexico City was fascinating to me. I learned a little Spanish so I could order a meal. We had a room at the YMCA, but Kibby left after about a week. He ran out of money. I had enough money to stay for a while, and the rate of exchange for the peso was 10 to 1 in my favor. I discovered that Americans at that time were a sought-after commodity, so, being outgoing myself, I had no trouble making friends. One night we wound up singing American songs in Spanish. I learned El Barrelito, the Beer Barrel Polka, accompanied by the Andrews Sisters. Occasionally I would go to the YMCA dances. The girls would line up on one side of the room with their "aunts "or in other words their chaperones, as required by the Spanish culture. I picked an attractive young lady, and after a few dances, she invited me to dinner at her parents home. I accepted. She lived in Chapultapec Heights, a pretty exclusive suburb of Mexico City. It turns out that her father was Mexican Ambassador to the Phillipines. I remember their dining room furniture. It was teakwood inlaid with ivory. The food was wonderful, but the budding romance did not last. Her family was called back to Manila.

Time went fast in Mexico City even though I was there for 2 months. I would go to the markets, visit historical sights (Mexico City is built in a huge volcanic crater), go to movies, write letters home, and to my girlfriend, Debbie. And on

Sundays I would go to the bullfights. One Sunday I saw a young lady named Conchita Cintron fight bulls from horseback. (I told that story to my friend Ron Giudicessi, and he wouldn't believe me.) In March of 2009, I opened the *Arizona Republic* and immediately saw a headline that read "Famed Woman Bullfighter Conchita Cintron Dies at 86." I sent the headline to Ron and a note that said, "Now do you finally believe me?" He has the article and note posted in his restaurant, Mezzodis. I don't advise going under the stands after the bullfights, which I did. They butcher the bull carcasses for sale, hence the saying, "Never eat beef on Monday in Mexico City".

My parents were wondering when I was coming home. I wrote that I was going to take a weekend trip to Acapulco, then I would return. The weekend turned into 3 months. I loved Acapulco, the sun, the sand, the beauty of the place. I was there when it was just an over-grown fishing village, not a mega-resort, although there were some lovely vacation spots even then. (El Mirador, next to where I was staying, was the place where Artie Shaw hid out after he famously left his band after the success of "Begin the Beguine"). There were a lot of Europeans in Acapulco at that time, because of the war, so we sort of had our own community. Days on the beach, evenings watching the gorgeous Pacific sunsets up at La Quebrada (the picturesque cliff you see them diving off of) then nights on the town. I loved it. But my parents didn't. They sent a friend down to talk to me. I realized it was time to go home.

If you had been at the Greyhound Bus Station in Des Moines on Christmas Eve Day, 1939, you would have seen this tall, slim guy, with a deeply tanned face and long blond hair, get off the bus, you would have seen me. Then it was back to Davenport and an exciting "Welcome Home." What a trip, what an experience. WOW! Now it was on to the next phase of my life; I was ready. My wanderlust had been taken care of, at least for a while. I felt that I had learned some practical lessons of life the past few months. Now I needed the lessons of the classroom.

MY KIND OF TOWN

Bill Wundram, the Bard of Davenport, wrote in *The Quad City Times* in 2005, "My town; it's a lovely place to live. At twilight, gazing at the old Gold Coast Mansions on the bluffs and church spires, the city looks absolutely Florentine. I keep saying it's a great town."

Wundram goes on, "At times, we may have needed reassurance, but we've always been strong and unafraid. Everyone was poor in the Great Depression, but we were poor with class. When there was a run on the Union Savings Bank, tuxedoed musicians from the Tri-City Symphony played in the lobby to calm hysterical depositors."

This hit home with me when I read it because my father was Executive Vice President of the Union Bank, during that "Run" by the depositors. He told me much later that he left the bank with 6 cents in his pocket that Christmas Eve in 1933.

My father also told me he was the one who hired those Symphony Musicians.

We were nothing if not resourceful back in those early Davenport days. We wanted to schedule a Christmas Holiday Dance, but all of the evening and afternoon dates were taken, so, why not a Breakfast Dance? That's what we did.

I co-hosted the affair with two high school chums, Jean Gehrmann and Marilyn Moritz. It made quite a hit. The *Davenport Democrat* ran a 2-column story and *The Daily Times* carried a 3-column article, both of them with photos. The *Democrat* reported "The Party was one of the most unique in the round-the-clock whirl of holiday events, arranged by the younger set. It was held in the Gold Room of Hotel Blackhawk, where some 200 guests danced to the music of Jack Manthey's Orchestra." Yes, indeed, we did have our social side in Davenport!

I love Davenport, and I am proud that Davenport saw fit to return the favor for a "Day".

City of Davenport, Iowa

PROCLAMATION

Whereas: Jim Zabel is a native of Davenport, Iowa, and a graduate of Davenport High School and the University of Iowa; and

Whereas: Jim became Iowa's most celebrated sportscaster and sports director of WHO, broadcasting more than 6,100 play-by-play events of the Iowa Barnstormers, University of Iowa basketball, six Rose bowl games, the Drake Relays, NCAA basketball tournaments, and every University of Iowa football game for 49 consecutive seasons; and

Whereas: Jim was named "Sportscaster of the Year", "I-Club Man of the Year", "Variety Club Sportsman of the Year", Variety Club Sportsman of the Year", and received the most prestigious honor in the radio industry, "Personality of the Year", by the National Association of Broadcasters; and

Now, Therefore, I, Charles W. Brooke, Mayor of the City of Davenport, Iowa hereby proclaim Saturday, May 15, 2004 as

JIM ZABEL DAY

And thank Jim for being a tireless champion for Davenport and the Quad Cities and Iowa.

_____
Charles W. Brooke, Mayor

EDUCATION 101: IOWA STYLE

Is there anything better than a college education?

I mean going away to a university, free of family problems and restrictions for the first time (but not family finances), breathing the fresh, pure air of academia, acquiring knowledge you never dreamed of, accepting challenges you never realized you could handle, going to the games and cheering the victories, finding the girl of your dreams, and just having a damn good time. Is that asking too much? That's the way I looked at it when I arrived on the campus in Iowa City.

I plunged right into undergraduate life. I pledged Sigma Chi fraternity, I signed up for a maximum number of class hours, I applied for a job as a reporter on The Daily Iowan, and I encountered Iowa track coach George Bresnahan as I was enrolling for my classes at Memorial Union.

He wanted me to go out for his track team and eventually receive a full scholarship. (He had seen a post-season meet in Cedar Rapids the year before where I won four first places. The meet pitted the Mississippi Valley Conference against the Little Six Conference, and I won the open 220- and 440-yard dashes, and anchored the winning 880 and mile relay teams.) I explained to him that things had changed since we last talked over a year before. I had been in an auto accident that banged up my right leg and did some nerve damage which affected my running. He didn't quite believe me and still wanted me to come out. (But it was true. My leg was operated on that fall by the renowned orthopedic surgeon, Dr. Steindler, after whom the hospital clinic at Iowa is named. It was successful, but I still didn't feel I could do justice to track). And truthfully, my priorities had changed. I realized I had to concentrate on my studies and my profession, which at that time was journalism.

I didn't feel I would have time for track. I no longer had Olympic stars in my eyes. There was too much to focus on—football games, social life with the Sigma Chis, dances at Memorial Union, my job on *The Daily Iowan*, and my studies. I hit the books hard that first semester, and was rewarded. I got the highest grades in the freshman class at my fraternity house, a collective A-minus.

I was a big football fan even then. My dad had taken me to a lot of Iowa games when I was a kid. I saw Ozzie Simmons, Joe Laws and Dick Crayne. I fell in love with the Iowa Hawkeyes. There weren't many victories back then (especially against the dreaded Minnesota Gophers), but it was fun.

One game I vividly remember a little later on (because I covered it for the *Iowan*) was the 1942 clash with Wisconsin. The Badgers were unbeaten, the #1 team in the Big 10 and one of the best in the country. They had three All-Americans—Elroy "Crazy Legs" Hirsch, Pat Harder and Dave Shreiner. Iowa had Tommy Farmer and the tough defensive coaching of Dr. Eddie Anderson.

The Hawkeyes won the hard-fought battle 6-0. It was a throwback to those heady days of Nile Kinnick three years before, when I was still in high school and then was in Mexico. I did interview Kinnick twice, at the Tribune All-Star Game in Chicago (where he played in 1940) and in the law library at Iowa, when he was in law school.

He was clean cut and athletic looking, but his size was not imposing. He stood about 5-feet-8 and probably weighed 175. With dark blond hair parted in the middle, and wearing a white v-neck sweater, he looked like a guy going out for a tennis match. He was probably 22 at the time, but he talked like a man 10 years older. He was, of course, a campus hero, but acted like he just wanted to be a student.

Years later, in fact, *Sports Illustrated* did a book-length article on him called "The Last True Scholar Athlete." That is the memory I kept of Nile Kinnick while I was working on the *Iowan*, first as Campus Editor, then Managing Editor, and in 1943 I became Editor-In-Chief.

Ensign Nile Kinnick, All-American '39, returns to scenes of former glory.

It was war time, and the military had taken over Iowa City. The Naval Pre-Flight school occupied the west side of the campus, and practically every other university building had some sort of military presence. Even East Hall, where the *Iowan* Editorial offices were located, was taken over by the Army Signal Corps. Our offices were in the basement, and every morning if I stayed there long enough after putting the paper to bed, I could hear the bugle blowing reveille over the loud speakers. (The story was that trumpeter Harry James recorded those bugle wake-up calls.)

It was with this atmosphere as background that we received the most dreaded news we could ever imagine. Nile Kinnick had been killed in a naval air crash in the Caribbean. It couldn't be true. It just couldn't. Not Nile Kinnick, the man many of us thought would be President some day. But—it was true.

Somehow, we managed to put out a paper. I don't know how, we were numb. We barely spoke. What I remember most is coming back to my office in East Hall (later Seashore Hall), and typing a letter to University President Virgil Hancher, suggesting that Iowa Stadium as soon as possible be named for Nile Kinnick. I said he was a legendary figure in the minds of all Iowans and deserved that kind of honor. Two days later I received a reply from President Hancher. He agreed with everything I said about Kinnick, but then added this: "Many men will lose their lives in World War II. Each of them deserves to be honored. I think it only prudent to wait until hostilities end before we make a final decision." In 1972, of course, the stadium was named for Nile Kinnick.

I loved my days on the *Iowan*. When I was editor, I wrote a column called "Editorially Speaking", which, in one readership survey, was named the second most popular feature in the paper. Number one was the comic strip "Blondie".

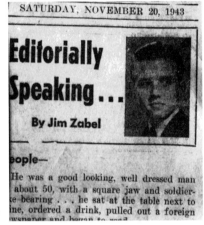

SATURDAY, NOVEMBER 20, 1943

Editorially Speaking . . .

By Jim Zabel

eople—

He was a good looking, well dressed man about 50, with a square jaw and soldier-e-bearing . . . he sat at the table next to ine, ordered a drink, pulled out a foreign

The column occasionally got me in hot water. In the summer of 1943, Dean Carl Seashore of the Graduate College and I published a collection of 12 Iowan essays entitled "Wartime Approaches to Liberal Education." It was a pretty lofty endeavor. The following fall, at Homecoming, I did a column on Iowa City's most popular student hangout, "The Central Tap", and its proprietor, Don Alberhasky. In the column I made the observation that former students returning to the campus visited Don at The Central Tap before they saw any of their professors.

The next day I received a sizzling letter from Dean Seashore. He accused me of appealing to the "lowest tastes of the community" by suggesting that students would rather visit with a "common bartender" than meet with the "academic leaders whose teachings had prepared them for life." I replied the next day by saying "okay, then why were there 3,000 people spilling on to the street at Central Tap, and only a security guard and maintenance man at Schaffer Hall?"

In my early days on the *Iowan,* I also did theater reviews. Some of them weren't too popular with the drama department. I reviewed one student production of Sheridan's Elizabethan comedy *School for Scandal,* which I pretty much panned. I wrote about "falsetto-voiced men with flaccid wrists chasing each other about the stage like schoolgirls." I said the play should have been called "School for Pansies." The UPI wire service picked up on it and it ran in newspapers around the Midwest.

Editor

JAMES ZABEL

The appointment of James Zabel, son of Fred W. Zabel, former Davenport banker, and Mrs Zabel, who now reside in Aurora, Ill., as editor of the Daily Iowan, University of Iowa student newspaper, was announced Wednesday. The former Davenporter was appointed by the board of student publications to succeed Robert Noble, Oelwein, who is now serving in the armed forces. Zabel is a junior in the college of liberal arts.

I paid a price for this. One night about a week later I was eating in Smith's Café when one of the leading actresses of the Iowa drama department, Martha Baird,

Youngest person to be named Editor, Daily Iowan in my junior year

spotted me. She grabbed me by the ear, marched me out of Smith's and into Joe's Tavern next door. She said "I want you to meet the actors you panned last week." There were about eight people seated around the table. I was flabbergasted by the whole thing. I explained, weakly I'm afraid, that I wasn't criticizing them, I was panning the affectations of the play. "Why don't you do something in this century?" I asked , hoping to get a laugh. They said they were. And they did. It was called "Barbara Allen", written by a local playwright and later made it to Broadway as "Dark of the Moon". I gave it a good review. But I discovered one thing, bad reviews get a lot more attention. However, it was nice to have peace in the ranks between me and the drama department.

I was a busy guy at Iowa. In addition to editing the *Iowan* and writing a daily column, I was taking 12 class hours, working a

I thought I owned the world when I worked on the Daily Iowan

board job at Delta Gamma Sorority, and was also doing a column about Davenport High students now at Iowa called "Red and Blue among the Gold". It ran in the *Davenport Daily Times* every Saturday.

My toughest decision as editor of the *Iowan* came on a winter day in 1943. Police reported findng the bodies of a young man and woman in a Coralville tourist cabin (that's what they called motels in those days because the rooms were actually separate units). They had been there for several days with a room temperature of 113 degrees caused by a faulty space heater. Then came the shocking news. The girl was queen of the junior nurse class at Iowa, and the man was president of the junior medical class. (I remember the names of both, but am not going to use them in consideration of their surviving families.) The man was married. The girl, who came from a prominent family in the East, was engaged to be married that June.

It was a sensational story, especially for that era. The complicating factor for me as a newspaper editor was this: That very day the Navy announced the sinking of the aircraft carrier Yorktown in the Pacific, with the loss of 1,800 lives. What to do? It was a dilemma I would have about one hour to solve. I talked it over with my managing editor, Jeanne Starr, then I gave her my decision: Banner the local story.

So, that's the way it came out on the front page of the Iowan the next morning. MEDIC, NURSE FOUND DEAD. In 96-point type, with two four-column cuts of the tourist cabin and the inside of the room on the front page (the Yorktown sinking was a sub banner).

I expected reaction, and it came fast. I got a call at 8 a.m. from my publisher, Fred Pownall. He wanted to see me "at once." He was my boss and we were both technically university employees. Pownall was burning. He had heard from the president and a number of other powers-that-be. Their stand was that as a publication of the university, we should consider the integrity and reputation of the university in our selection of stories. "In other words," I said "protect the university, right?" Pownhall hemmed and hawed a bit. I went on, "I was always told by my instructors that we were a city newspaper, not just a university paper, and every news editing course I have taken says the big local story takes precedence over the big national story." I am not sure I won my case, but I made my point and managed to keep my job. Privately, I think Fred Pownall agreed with me.

The autopsy results came down several weeks later. The ruling, rendered by Dean Teeters of the University Medical School, who was also State Toxicologist, was "accidental death."

My curiosity was not completely satisfied with the facts of the case as I knew them. Neither were the dead girl's parents. They hired two Pinkerton detectives to investigate, and I spent a full afternoon with one of them. He told me something unusual. The hood of the man's car was raised, and alcohol had been

1942, University of Iowa:
Hew Roberts (left), visiting lecturer from Australia, Jim Zabel (center),
Chairman, Victory Rally Committee, President Virgil Hancher (right)

removed from the radiator, (there was no anti-freeze in those days, alcohol was used in the winter).

The case remained a mystery. Then some 30 years later, I happened to be visiting with a doctor friend one night at the Athletic Club. Somehow the tourist cabin case came up. He told me that as an undergraduate medical student at the university he had been an intern at the autopsy of the girl. "I know the verdict was accidental death," he said "and that was technically correct. But what we found out was that the girl was three months pregnant, and we suspected the man was trying to perform an abortion, using alcohol from the radiator in his car. They were both overcome by fumes from the space heater, and that's how they died."

So, in a way the university achieved the protection from publicity it thought it deserved, but I also realized my desire to solve the mystery of the case. This is the first time true details have been made public. So.......case closed.

All of our work on the Iowan, and there many more big stories we covered in depth, paid off for us. The *Iowan* won an award

Daily Iowan staff celebrate after work

for "Excellence" at the Iowa Newspaper Publishers Convention in Des Moines. It was a proud moment when I stepped into the Grand Ballroom of the Fort Des Moines Hotel to accept it.

Because of my work on the *Iowan*, I attended three summer sessions at Iowa, meaning that I was able to finish in three-and-a-half years.

In August of 1943, I spent a week in New York City, job hunting and enjoying the sights. My cousin from Davenport was Otis Weise, Editor and Publisher of *McCalls Magazine*, (he was one of those boy wonders who got the job at the age of 23, directly out of the University of Wisconsin.) He insisted that I stay in his suite at the Waldorf Astoria, and he took me to places like the Ritz Men's Bar, 21 Club and the Stork Club. I met people like Hollywood Producer Hunt Stromberg, Author Louis Bromfield and New Yorker Film Critic George Jean Nathan, among others. I also had a lot of job interview doors opened for me. I talked with editors of *Life Magazine, Look Magazine* and the *New York Herald Tribune,* and received written job offers from all three.

So my sights were set. New York was the place! The excitement and anticipation were overpowering. I had even lined up an apartment with Bob Phieffer, a former roommate at Iowa who had just gotten an announcing job at CBS.

Then the U.S. Army entered my life again. My draft board in Iowa City, which originally classified me 4-F because of my auto accident injuries, had reclassified me 1-B, meaning I could be called anytime.

I contacted the board, and they advised me to stay in the Midwest. So, I went to my parents home in Aurora, Ill., just outside of Chicago, where my father had become Vice President of Merchants National Bank.

Through various contacts in Chicago, I got in touch with one of the top radio producers there named Les Weinrott. He wrote three daily radio soap operas and network specials. He said he needed a writer for a new show he was doing on CBS called "America in the Air". It was sponsored by Wrigley and told the stories of Air Force pilots who had flown missions in Europe and the Pacific. He wanted me to submit a sample script. I wrote one in 7 days. It was about 2 pilots from Aurora who I had read about, and their exploits over Italy. I called it "Fortress over Foggia."

Weinrott liked it and hired me. He gave me a private office on Wacker Drive in downtown Chicago and told me to clean out the desk drawers.

I found scripts with actors like Tyrone Power, Don Ameche, John Garfield and John Hodiak, all of whom had worked for him in Chicago before going to Hollywood. In the ensuing months, I helped to interview pilots, prepare their stories for the air, and write some of the dialogue for the show, which ran on 468 CBS stations.

I learned a lot about writing from Weinrott, especially script writing, "Never put a line on paper," he said, "unless it's funny or moves the story ahead". He also talked about using power words in writing to music (we had a full studio orchestra on "America in the Air") such as "The Surging of the Giant Fortress Engines". He was demanding to work for, but I was fascinated with his talent. He could dictate a script to music, which is tough to do.

"America in the Air" was broadcast from the WBBM studios in the Wrigley Building. I got to know some of the actors on the show. One was Peter Flynn, who played "Jack Armstrong, The All-American Boy" on weekdays. People today think of New York and Los Angeles as being the centers of the TV world, but back in those radio days it was Chicago. Almost all of the big network radio shows originated in the Windy City.

We met with sponsors and actors and producers. One time at the Wrigley Building we had lunch with Phil Wrigley and Gene Autry, who was planning a radio show with us.

And so it went. But I discovered something. I wanted to do more than write. I wanted to get on "the other side of the mike". My chance came when Jack Shelley, news director of WHO, visited our office. He had known Weinrott earlier in the war, when Les had spent time in Des Moines. Jack said he would like to talk to me. I told him I was going back to Iowa City to pick up my diploma at spring graduation (I had taken my last six hours at Iowa by correspondence.) Shelley asked "Why don't you come to Des Moines?" I said I would. I didn't know then, but I was about to begin a lifelong journey to a destination of unbelievable possibilities.

The University of Iowa
Department of Anatomy

DATE... May 24, 1971 ....

TO... Jim Zabel .... FROM... Clarence G. Strub ...

I have always considered your December 9,
1943 Daily Iowan editorial to be one of the
finest pieces of writing I have ever read.
A few days ago I sent a copy of it to the
Daily Iowan with the suggestion that they
try to learn to write as well. It appears
that they liked it too...see page 2 of the
attached. Here you are back in the D.I. after
almost thirty years.

Clarence

Clarence G. Strub

Public Relations

Department of Anatomy

Chapter 2

WHO Stole My Heart Away

A Fine Romance

CONFESSIONS OF A BUDDING BROADCASTER

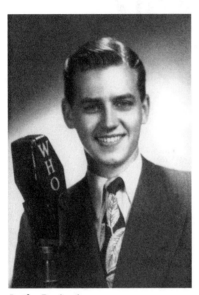

In the Beginning...

Even though I had worked in Chicago as a script writer at CBS, coming to WHO was something special for me. I had listened to WHO since I was a kid, and although Reagan had left by this time, I knew all the rest of the personalities by heart—Jack Shelley, the renowned newsman, Jack Kerrigan (star of "Melody Madhouse"), announcer Bobby Griffin, entertainers like Slim Hayes, Lucia Thorne, Cliff & Helen, Lem & Martha, and pianists Bill Austin and Eddie Scoffield. (Andy Williams and Roger Williams were just starting their careers on WHO).

The "WHO Barn Dance Frolic," broadcast live every Saturday night, ranked right behind "The Grand Ole Opry" out of Nashville, in popularity. General Manager Joe Maland brought the programming plan with him when he came from WLS in Chicago. WHO historian Jen Jack said, "We were almost like a third network, right behind NBC and CBS, because our WHO signal gave us a huge national audience, as well as a local one."

My first day on the job was May 18, 1944. Shelley put me to work immediately writing for his noon newscast, which was the highest rated news program in the state during those war years. My first on-air appearance, several weeks later, occurred almost by accident, and I felt it was a disaster, although others found it amusing. Farm Director Herb Plambeck asked me to do the noon markets which was foreign territory for me. I was doing fine, and thought I was home free, until I came to the Chicago Stock Yards. The copy read "Sheep and Ewes", but by my city-boy interpretation it came out "Sheep and EE-WEES". Needless to say, the farm guys never let me hear the end of that.

My career took off over the next few months as I began doing all the things I dreamed of doing, like sportscasts, interviews and special events, in addition to newscasts.

Shelley asked me to do a Sunday noon interview show called "Speaking of People." Some of my guests included Bob Hope, Jimmy Stewart, Ronald Reagan, British Prime Minister Anthony Eden, Jack Dempsey, Jane Fonda, former President Herbert Hoover and Jerry Lewis, plus a lot of other people from all walks of life. It turned out to be a very popular show and ran for years.

About that time I also landed a sports show called "Standard Oil Spotlight." This show featured musical numbers by The Song-fellows and a female vocalist and high intensity sports segment which I would lead into by saying in my best play-by-play voice "This is Jim Zabel, your Standard Oil Sportscaster, training the spotlight on sports". When I went on vacation, announcer Del Donahoo was assigned to fill in. He asked me what to watch out for. I told him you really had to be fired up, like you're

Here is where it all started...

In the beginning, I also did the 10 o'clock news on WHO-TV

doing a game, but be careful you don't trip up on the lead-in lines. Of course, that got Del, a natural worrier, to thinking. Maybe too much.

You know how it came out, don't you? On his very first night, he said "This is Del Donahoo, your Standard Oil Sportscaster, training the sportlight on spots!" After that, he tip-toed his way through the opening. (I think it was on that same broadcast that announcer Archie Leonard referred to Standard Oil Gasoline "With its higher volitilititty.") Talk about maneuvering your way through verbal minefields.

That's what happened to me when I was assigned my first newscast on WHO. It was Sunday morning at 10 o'clock. That was tough enough since I had to be there by 8 a.m. to prepare my copy. But the toughest part was my sponsor, Funk G. Hybrid Seed Corn. They insisted that I come on cold after the 10 o'clock break and following a dramatic pause, say in my most booming voice "Funk! F-U-N-K, the greatest name in hybrid seed corn, presents the 10 o'clock news": The possibility of a slip up being what it was, I heaved a sigh of relief when I made it through the opening. My first story was of a new marine landing in the Pacific. I said "The Netherlecks have landed", then as panic set in, I tried to correct myself, and practically shouted "Netherlecks!...Netherlecks!! Somehow, I managed to regain my composure, and finished the newscast, but I pointedly used the name "Marines" in place of Leathernecks.

By the late 1940's I was doing practically everything I was hired to do and more—newscasts, sportscasts, straight announcing and special events. I even wrote some scripts for "Melody Madhouse."

But the one thing I wanted most to do was play-by-play football and basketball. However, that possibility had not been viable because virtually all live sports coverage, particularly Iowa football, had been suspended during the war. Now it was back on the schedule again, generating a lot of interest among our listeners, who remembered the glory days of Ronald Reagan. It also generated considerable competition among the members of

Interviewing Vicki Draves, a great Olympic diver for the United States

our announcing staff, most of whom—by virtue of age alone, had more experience than me.

In the spring of 1949, I had recorded some play-by-play highlights of the Drake Relays which were replayed that night. They say that luck is the combination of preparation and opportunity. My preparation was the fact that I had competed in the Drake Relays myself and knew a lot about the athletes I was covering. My opportunity was the fact that since it was broadcast at night, a lot of the Front Office heard it.

Two days later my luck paid off. Vice President Woody Woods called me into his office and said those magic words that I will never forget—"You're going to be doing Iowa football next fall." I was dumbfounded and elated at the same time. I felt like I had reached the pinnacle—the same way Reagan must have felt those many years ago when—like me, with no actual play-by-play experience—he was hired to do the Iowa games. With WHO's tremendous coverage, it was like being on a network broadcast.

Now the hard part started. I made many trips to Iowa City that summer, talking with coaches and players. (It was Eddie Anderson's last year). In August of that year I made a 2,000 mile trip by car around the Big 10, visiting all of the football camps, interviewing coaches and players, watching practice and getting background facts from Sports Information Directors. Some of the head coaches of that era were Bernie Bierman of Minnesota, Fritz Crisler of Michigan, Biggie Munn of Michigan State, Wes Fesler of Ohio State (Woody's predecessor) and Ray Eliot of Illinois. These were all tough, hard-nosed guys who knew how to produce champions (Minnesotans liked to tell a story about Bierman's recruiting. As he drove down a country road in Minnesota, he would spot a kid in a field and would ask him to point the direction to the next town. If the kid pointed, Bierman would thank him. If the kid picked up the plow and pointed, Bierman would recruit him).

Iowa's Eddie Anderson was out of the same mold as his Big 10 contemporaries. A practicing surgeon, Anderson would come directly from the operating room to the football field.

The big moment finally arrived—the first game of the 1949 season and my debut as "The Voice of Hawkeye Football." The opponent was UCLA at Iowa Stadium. (It wasn't named for Kinnick until 1972). The Bruins proved to be too much, winning 41-25.

How did the first broadcast go? Pretty well, I thought, but a little rough around the edges. Play-by-play is difficult. It's like describing an auto accident happening. When a guy breaks over right tackle and goes 75 yards for a touchdown, your normal reaction is to shout "WOW—look at that!" Instead, you've got to describe it, and your color man has to fill in the blocking assignments.

Gradually, I developed my own play-by-play style—and I will have to admit I incorporated quite a bit of the "WOW" factor in with the factual description because I have always felt I represented the fan at the game.

Cover from the 1937 WHO Picture Book

Whatever the reasoning behind it, our Iowa Football ratings were phenomenal. On one survey, we had more audience than the next five leading stations combined. I will be the first to admit that a lot of the credit for the success of our football and basketball broadcasts goes to the color analysts who worked with me, most recently Ed Podolak and Bobby Hansen. I hired them both. They are the best.

What do I most remember out of that first season in 1949? The Oregon game on October 29. Iowa trailed 28-7 going into the fourth quarter, and more than half of the fans had left the stadium, then, as if by magic, Bill Reichardt ran a kickoff back 100 yards for a touchdown. Don Longly scored on a 90 yard punt return. The Hawks scored two more times, incredibly, to win 34–31. Most fans heard the fourth quarter on their car radios, and could hardly believe what had happened.

Not everything was peaches and cream in those early days. Our biggest sponsor, Standard Oil (later Amoco) was not happy with the Hawkeyes losing record (4 wins in 1948, 4 in 1949, 3 in 1950, 2 in 1951). Since our signal covered the entire Midwest and more, Standard Oil wanted to do a "Big 10 Game of the Week".

I attended an urgent meeting of the Standard Oil top brass in Mason City. Presiding over the meeting was Standard Oil District Manager Col. Day (interestingly, he was the father of the Day twins, Pee Wee and Fats, who hold the distinction of having played on two state championship high school basketball teams—at Davenport and Mason City, in two different years). Col. Day was a man of military bearing, who was definitely in command, but he was fair with me. I pleaded my case on an emotional basis, saying that Iowa fans wanted to hear the Hawkeyes, win or lose, because they loved their team, their university, and their state, and they had great loyalty to the products we advertised while broadcasting the Hawkeyes. I stressed that Standard Oil was important because their sponsorship enabled us to carry the games. I won them over. Standard Oil continued as our main sponsor.

From these early beginnings, our WHO sports coverage grew into a giant play-by-play machine, as large as any 50,000 watt station in the country, and bigger than most.

There was a time, back in the 1960's and 70's, when we broadcast basketball games of Drake and Iowa State, as well as Iowa, sometimes doing triple-header and double-header games on nights where the schedules conflicted. Then there were the Boys' and Girls' State Basketball Tournaments, which we did from start to

The University of Iowa Marching Band Salutes WHO

1960s in studio

finish. In 1970, I did a total of 126 basketball games on WHO, including Iowa, Drake, Iowa State and the Boys' and Girls' tournaments. (The *Des Moines Register* did a cover story on me at that time called "The Talking Machine on Channel 13.")

The tremendous coverage of WHO (border to border and coast to coast) was a major reason for our success, and paid many dividends. At one time I was doing Iowa basketball games with Des Moines Savings and Loan as a sponsor. One of their commercials had this tagline—"If you can't make it to Des Moines Savings and Loan, send your check to me and I will personally deposit it for you." Believe it or not, I received checks as high as $15,000 made out to me personally. One check for $7,000 came from a listener in Ketchikan, Alaska, who had never been to the state of Iowa. (We built a radio and TV commercial around that one).

Another letter came from a listener in Detroit named Roy Karro. He said he was a big Iowa fan and appreciated the broadcasts so much he was going to make a donation to the University of Iowa. That he did—3 million dollars to build the new Iowa Hall of Fame, which bears his name. I was there for the ribbon cutting, and personally thanked Roy.

Our extended coverage of Hawkeye football actually began in 1956, Iowa's first Rose Bowl year. Our General Manager, Paul Loyet, came to me with an idea. He said Iowa fans on the West Coast were complaining that they couldn't get enough coverage of Hawkeye games, so why didn't we do a re-broadcast at night, when our signal came booming into California and all points west. I said I thought it was great idea, and so we

Jeanette Olson and Denise Long hug after the 1968 game

Photo printed with permission by the Des Moines Register

started something that was revolutionary for its time and was a huge success. The rebroadcast soundly out-rated everything against it, and the fans included coaches Joe Paterno of Penn State and Barry Switzer of Oklahoma, both of whom told me they were regular listeners.

I have many fond memories of the five Rose Bowl games I broadcast with the Hawkeyes, and more than 30 NCAA Tournaments. And how can I ever forget that sensational battle between Denise Long and Jeanette Olson in the most celebrated girls basketball game of all time in 1968.

The color, the pageantry, the thrill of being able to be at the microphone through it all.

I LOVE IT…I LOVE IT…I LOVE IT…

Working with Randy Duncan (middle) and Gary Fletcher (right)

Chapter 3

FOOTBALL DAYS

IOWA SPEED ROUTS CAL, 38-12
Jeter Races 81 for Touchdown, Totals 194 Yards for Rose Bowl Records

IOWA ROMPS IN ROSE BOWL, 35-19
Ploen Runs 49 at Start, Hagler Gallops 66 Against Oregon State

THE BIG PEACH
Hawkeyes win No. 1 thriller, 12-10

SPORTS
Long, Hawkeyes shred Texas, 55-17

Historic Headlines and the Men Who Made Them

EVY
TURBULENT GENIUS

"How did you manage to get along with Forest Evashevski?" a newcomer to the Iowa media asked. "Was your relationship based on respect, admiration or adultation"?

"Try fear," I replied with very little tongue-in-cheek.

Nothing was more chilling than Evashevski's voice on the phone at 8 a.m.

I know.

In 1954, I was negotiating with him for an exclusive Iowa Football show on WHO-TV. He had verbally agreed in the spring of that year to do a one-hour Sunday night film show, live from our TV studios in Des Moines. Our sales department immediately signed a flock of sponsors, including some very heavy hitters of that era. By August, however, I still had not received a signed contract from Evashevski. I went to see him in Chicago, where he was serving as one of the coaches for the Tribune All-Star Football Game. Confronting him in the lobby of the Sherman Hotel, I found he had become reluctant about certain aspects

Mr. Evashevski

of the show pertaining to what revenue went where (the tug-of-war with Athletic Director Paul Brechler had already begun). I was in a panic. The first show was less than four weeks away, and the "star" was still unsigned.

I came back to Des Moines and wrote him a stinging letter, accusing him, in effect, of backing out on something he had already agreed to.

Three days later the answer came. The phone at my home rang at 8 a.m. and my wife said, "It's Evashevski."

I said, "Hello." Then came the words that went through me like cold steel.

"I didn't like the tone of your damn letter!" Evashevski said, with the deep resonance that only his voice could convey.

I guess my response, as I remember it, approximated Groucho Marx's reply when someone asked him, "Are you a man or a mouse?" and he said, "Throw a piece of cheese on the floor and you'll find out." At any rate, I emerged from the conversation with a contract, or promise thereof (on which he delivered), and I began a long relationship with the young Iowa coach in which I managed to survive and, comparatively speaking, to thrive.

I looked at Evashevski then as probably the most fascinating, complex and talented man I had ever met—a man so driven to succeed that nothing that stood in his way would remain there long. In fact, that was the premise of a 6,000 word story I did on Evashevski in 1957, which *TRUE* (the top-selling men's magazine of that era) ran as their lead article in November of that year, under the title of "Football Firebrand". In that article, I quoted Fritz Crisler, Evy's coach at Michigan, as saying, "Evashevski was the toughest, most determined and most intelligent player I ever coached." Once you understood this toughness, this stopping at nothing to succeed, you understood Evashevski, or at least what fueled his emotional drive. I once introduced him at a Greater Des Moines Chamber of Commerce luncheon with, "Forest Evashevski has often been called ruthless and insensitive. I just want you to know that beneath that cold exterior there beats a heart of stone."

Evy was a bulldozer, not a compromiser. George Wine, Iowa Sports Information Director Emeritus, tells of the time the

President's office called requesting 40 parking passes for Saturday's game. Wine said he couldn't authorize that many and would have to run the request by Evy. When he walked into Evashevski's office, he was reading a magazine.

Wine said, "Evy, the President's office called. They want 40 parking passes for Saturday's game."

Without looking up, Evashevski replied, "F___ 'em."

Evy's attitude toward the media was equally direct. "If you're winning, you don't need 'em. If you're losing, they can't help you."

Actually, Evashevski got along very well with the media while he was coaching. He was young, dynamic, outspoken—and he was a winner. Almost any subject brought out his sense of humor.

One day, a reporter asked him how he liked the new Cadillac the alumni had given him after Iowa's 1957 Rose Bowl victory.

"It's great," Evy replied. "Except when I went into a gas station yesterday and told the attendant to 'fill it up', he said 'shut off the engine and give me a fighting chance.'"

On another occasion, I was walking by Evy's office in the Field House with Gus Schrader, sports editor of the Cedar Rapids Gazette. Gus had just done a story about Evy giving up cigarettes in favor of chewing tobacco. As we passed Evy's office, Gus leaned in and asked if it was true that he and his wife, Ruth, were expecting their sixth child. Evy replied, "First, you're investigating my chewing, now you're investigating my screwing."

Evashevski's wit was keen even as a player. During World War II, when his old running mate at Michigan, the legendary Tom Harmon, was rescued in China after being downed behind enemy lines, Evashevski wired him: "How did you make it back without me to block for you?"

(Some 50 years later, upon being inducted into the Michigan Hall of Honor, Evashevski remarked, "Harmon always said that without him I would have been just another unpronounceable Polish name.")

Addressing a booster meeting at Iowa shortly after his hiring, Evy said, "We're going to have a football team at Iowa even if I have to dip into the student body to get it." On another occasion, after he had said "I don't have to coach. I've got a rich father-in-law." he said his father-in-law wired him, "You better win! I don't have that much money!" (His father-in-law was Prentiss Brown, OPA Director in World War II, then later U.S. Senator and president of the Detroit Edison Co.) Evashevski could project toughness, wit, charm and intellect almost at the same moment. "I've never known a man who could dominate a room like he can!" said a prominent Iowa booster of that time. And Evy's coterie of friends numbered some of the wealthiest and most powerful men in the state—Governor Harold Hughes, Joe Rosenfield and Bob Root of Des Moines, George Foerstner of Amana, Howard Hall of Cedar Rapids, George Marguiles of Davenport—to mention just a few, whose support became the backbone of the rebuilding of the Iowa Football program. His attractiveness to these men was really quite simple. He embodied the same qualities they most admired in business, and, perhaps, themselves. "Powerful men like powerful men," one of Evashevski's followers of that day said. "And Evy is the epitome of power." No question about that—after all, here was a man who taught hand-to-hand combat to pre-flight cadets in World War II, and before that was one of the most punishing blocking backs in the history of college football. (There is no denying Evashevski's attractiveness to women, also. More than one referred to his "animal magnetism". One social arbiter of the time compared him to Clark Gable: "Men wanted to take him hunting—women wanted to take him home.")

Evashevski's tenure at Iowa (it's hard to believe he coached only nine years and retired at age 42) can be broken into three segments: 1) Building (1952-55); 2) Success (1956-60), and 3) Bitterness (1961-70). All three of these periods of Iowa

Football history have been well chronicled by just about every-one who covered the Evashevski years, and depending on who you talk to or read, you can get almost any opinion you want; especially so the last segment of the Evashevski era. No one denies the rapture of the first nine years of his regime—two Rose Bowl victories and a place in the top 10 teams in the nation five of the nine years. Euphoria swept the state. With the exception of a few moments of glory in 1921-22 with the Howard Jones-Duke Slater teams, and in 1939 with Nile Kin-nick and the immortal Ironmen, Iowa had not played winning football in half a century. "What Evashevski's teams did for the pride of the state was unbelievable," the late Francis "Buzz" Graham (former Hawkeye ticket manager) said. "Going to the Rose Bowl for the first time, winning the Big 10, being ranked among the top teams in the nation—this was all new to us, and it made us feel like special people."

Mike Chapman, publisher of the *Iowa History Journal* and an Evashevski biographer, wrote, "Forest Evashevski's impact on the University of Iowa and on the entire state was staggering. He came to a coaching graveyard in 1952 and he brought not only respectability but overwhelming success. Pride was a by-prod-uct of the Evashevski era, and it was a pride that would be felt the length and width of the state. For nine long years, Iowans could walk proud in the fabled area of collegiate athletics. Perhaps no other endeavor, rightly or wrongly, provides a state with a greater sense of awareness and well-being than does collegiate sports."

Evashevski's life was not all Xs & Os. He was an accomplished bridge player, he was adept at the piano and organ, and he was an ardent hunter and fisherman. He couldn't wait for the pheasant season to begin, although his hunting was restricted by his football priorities. He and his wife Ruth raised seven children. One of his closest friends was Joe Rosenfield, CEO of Younkers and a confidant of Warren Buffet. Joe and I often trav-eled on the same flights to road games. He told me, "Evy has a mind like a steel trap. He's a great businessman." Indeed, he was. He invested in shopping centers around the country and

In 1952, after the upset of the decade against Ohio State
Photo printed with permission by the Des Moines Register

in real estate both in Florida and Iowa. He was on the board of
directors of at least one bank and insurance company. Evy told
me that one time he tipped Rosenfield off about a good stock
deal in a Michigan bank. He told Joe, "They have 10,000 shares
left." Rosenfield said he wasn't interested. About a month
later Evy decided that he himself would buy up the remaining
shares. Evy said, "I called the bank and they told me the investment was no longer available. They told me 'some guy from
Des Moines named Rosenfield bought all 10,000 shares.'"

Iowa's football "Camelot" really began in 1956, when Evashevski installed the Wing-T Formation, which he himself
helped to invent. To be sure, there were memorable victories
before that—the 8-0 "Upset of the Decade" over Ohio State in
1952 (Evy changed the undermanned Hawkeye offense from
the Single-Wing to the Split-T in one week's time); the 14-14 tie
with #1 Notre Dame in 1953, amid charges of Irish skulldug-
gery which many feel cost Frank Leahy his job as head coach
(prompting Evy's famous post-game poetry: "When the one
great scorer comes to write against your name, he writes not
whether you won or lost, but how come we got gypped at Notre

Dame.") But 1956 was really when the big turnaround took place. The amazing Hawkeyes, spearheaded by Kenny Ploen and young quarterback Randy Duncan, raced through an 8-1 season to a 35-19 win over Oregon State in the Rose Bowl.

Evy always said the key game in the 1956 season was Purdue at West Lafayette. Iowa won that game 21–20, but at the end Purdue Quarterback Lenny Dawson was driving down the field with about two minutes to play when he threw a pass to his big tight end Lamar Lundy. The ball slipped through his fingers and onto the ground. Iowa Captain John Nocera fell on top of it. Purdue coaches screamed that it was an incomplete pass, but the refs ruled it was a fumble, recovered by Iowa. Years later, in the '90s, Podolak and I were doing an Iowa-Purdue game at West Lafayette, and I was recounting my memories of the '56 game to Podolak. He said, "I don't remember it. I was six years old." Then he added, "But I'll call a guy who does remember it." With that, Podolak had our engineer place a call right on the air. It was to Lenny Dawson in Kansas City. (Podolak played with him, of course, on the Kansas City Chiefs) "Leonard," Podolak said, "we're in beautiful Ross-Ade Stadium in West Lafayette—a place that I know you remember. My friend here, Jim Zabel, wants to know if you remember that 1956 game with Iowa?" Dawson said, "I'll never forget it." I asked, "How about that pass to Lundy, and the fumble?" Dawson really got his hackles up. "That was no fumble! That was an incompletion! We should have won the game!" I said to Podolak, "Great players never forget, do they?"

"The Wing-T caught everyone by surprise," Randy Duncan said later. "No one could defense it, and it took five years for them to figure out how to stop it." Blending together key elements of the Single-Wing and T-Formation, with pulling linemen and misdirection plays, the Wing-T baffled opponents for the rest of the 1950s. Former Minnesota Coach Bernie Bierman, himself the architect of five national championships with the Gophers, called Evy's 1958 club "the best offensive team I have ever seen." This team led the Big 10 in total offense and set four all-time

Rose Bowl records in a 38-12 win over California on January 1, 1959. (Esco Sarkkinen, Woody Hayes' top assistant at Ohio State, called the Wing-T the "East-West" offense because of the criss-crossing backs and pulling linemen. He also told me one time "you've got to have 25% better material to beat Evy's teams.") The stars of those Evashevski teams included some of the greatest players in Iowa history: Alex Karras, Calvin Jones, Jim Gibbons, Frank Gilliam, Bobby Jeter, John Nocera, Frank Rigney, Willie Fleming, Gary Grouwinkel, Jerry Hilgenberg, Don Norton, Curt Merz, in addition to Ploen and Duncan.

Evy was obsessed with beating Michigan. "He wanted to beat his alma mater more than anybody," Randy Duncan said. "I remember when they had Ron Kramer, who was the toughest, strongest and meanest guy in the Big 10. Kramer played defensive end. Evy said 'we're going to run our off-tackle play at him all day, until he has blood coming from his mouth and eyes and ears.' So we did. We ran our biggest back, Don Dobrino, play after play. Kramer stuffed him every time. I don't think we made 10 yards against him all day!"

So, how did Evashevski react to Kramer? After all, here was the guy who almost single-handedly beat his Hawkeyes.

When Kramer (a multiple sport athlete) came to Iowa City with the Michigan basketball team that winter, guess where he spent his game-day afternoon? You guessed it. At Evashevski's house. I found that out from Evy himself. "I love the kid," Evy said. "He's a hell of a player."

So, it's true. Great coaches admire great players, regardless of team colors. (And if the colors happen to be those of your alma mater, do you think that may help?)

I remember the annual Big 10 Banquet at the Rose Bowl, held in the Biltmore Hotel and emceed by Bob Hope. In 1956, Hope's opening line was: "The first time I heard of Forest Evashevski I thought it was a park in Russia." Then Hope introduced Jayne Mansfield with: "Here she is boys, 38-26-34....hike!" Sophomore

Randy Duncan was selected by Hope to come up from the audience and to kiss Mansfield. When Randy (on cue) held the embrace a little too long, Hope said: "Don't make a meal out of it, liver lips." In 1958 Hope, who had just returned from his traditional overseas Christmas visit with American troops, said: "I want to thank the Army for getting me here so that I could be with you tonight. They flew me back in a plane that belonged to a four-star general—Pershing." (Incidentally, when Hope was honored in 1991 as "Man of the Years" for his many appearances at the Big 10 banquets, it was Hayden Fry and Bump Elliott who flew to Los Angeles to present the award. Both have had a long-time friendship with Hope, Hayden's dating from his years at SMU.)

These were, indeed, heady days for Iowa fans. During one four-year span, 1955 through 1958, Iowa went to the Rose Bowl twice and won both games; the Hawkeye basketball team, under Bucky O'Connor, went to back-to-back Final Fours; Jack Fleck, my old classmate at Davenport High School (he captained the golf team the same year I captained the track team, 1939) won the U.S. Open Golf Tournament in a playoff with Ben Hogan; and Carol Morris of Ottumwa won the Miss Universe contest.

Evashevski was a master psychologist. (After all, he majored in psychology at Michigan, and in his senior year he won the Big 10 scholarship medal.) There are many stories of Evy's ability to "get into the heads" of his players. After one particularly sluggish practice, Evy berated the team in no uncertain terms. Then in the locker room he treated them to an ice cream, cake and pop party. The next practice was the best of the season.

It was a bitter cold day in Minneapolis when the Iowa team bus arrived at Memorial Stadium. The security guard said he couldn't let them in without the proper credentials. He said they would have to walk around to the other side of the stadium if they wanted to get in. So they got out and started walking, getting madder by the minute. Iowa beat Minnesota 7 to 0 that day and went on to win the 1956 Big 10 title. Incidentally, at the end of the game, Evashevski still had the credentials in his pocket.

Iowa was a heavy favorite over California in the 1959 Rose Bowl game, and Evy was worried about complacency. Suddenly, in the final week of practice it was announced that a California scout had been watching the Hawkeye workouts. "He was stealing our signals," Evy said. "We had to change everything." So the Hawkeyes revised their snap counts and play calls, which meant a lot of extra work. I rode to the game on the team bus, and the players were steaming. Iowa won the 1959 Rose Bowl game 38-12, setting 4 all-time records in the process, including a record-breaking average of 23 yards a carry by Bobby Jeter.

Alex Karras and Forest Evashevski were oil and water. Not only did they not get along, they hated each other. They did not speak for 50 years. Evy kicked him off the team, but he came back and became one of the Iowa all-time greats. He was an All-American, a runner up for the Heisman, and All-Pro for many years in the NFL. When I had him on my radio show in 2009, Alex put it very simply—"Evy made a man out of me."

I can't deny that covering the Rose Bowl is a thrill. You are constantly rubbing elbows with celebrities. I was standing in front of the team hotel in Pasadena, the Huntington Sheraton, when NBC-TV announcer Mel Allen came by and asked to pick my mind about Evy's Wing-T, since he would be doing the Rose Bowl game. As we were talking, "Wizard of Oz" star Ray Bolger came by. Turns out, he was a Big 10 fan. After that, Michigan Athletic Director Fritz Crisler joined us. Allen asked him where he was going to sit during the game since he had coached both Evy and

California's Pete Elliott. Crisler said, "I'll probably spend more time in the California section. I think Pete needs more help."

The romance of the Evashevski era extended through the 1960 season, when Iowa played Minnesota for the Big 10 and National Championship in Minneapolis—a bitter, bruising ballgame won by the Gophers 27-10. The disappointment of that loss was compounded by the fact that the Gophers were chosen by the Big 10 to represent the conference in the Rose Bowl. This despite the fact that Minnesota lost the following week to Wisconsin, while Iowa was handing Ohio State a resounding 35-10 whipping in Iowa City, the most lopsided Iowa win in the history of the series.

After the 1960 season, Evashevski had a choice to make—perhaps the most important choice in modern Iowa Football history. The Iowa Board in Control of Athletics, the governing body of Hawk-eye sports, told Evy the year before (following the departure of embattled Athletic Director Paul Brechler) that he could serve as coach and athletic director for one season, 1960—after that, he had to choose one or the other. Board members stated privately they were afraid of concentrating "too much power" in the hands of one man. Evashevski countered by saying he needed total control over the football program if the university hoped to

continue the kind of football prominence he had led it to during the 1950s. This standoff, preceded and followed by much pushing and pulling by the pro-and-con Evashevski factions behind the scenes, resulted in a decision that turned out to be tragic from just about everyone's standpoint—most of all, the

Paul Brechler and Forest Evashevski
Photo printed with permission by the Des Moines Register

Iowa football fans. Evashevski chose to become full-time Athletic Director, giving up the coaching reins to Assistant Jerry Burns. Looking back over the roughly 50 years since that decision was made, and trying to evaluate it, the fact becomes more and more apparent that, regardless of whose responsibility it was and regardless of who succeeded Evashevski as a coach, this single act not only opened the door to years of turmoil in and out of the athletic department, but cost Iowa the chance to remain a national football power.

"Iowa was on the threshold of being Nebraska," one knowledgeable football man of the time put it. "Instead they voted to remain Iowa." That judgement may be too harsh, and perhaps over-simplified, but it edges pretty close to the truth. Had Evashevski stayed as coach, or had the Board granted his wish to be coach-athletic director, there is no question Iowa would have remained the kind of national power it had become in the late 1950s—the recruiting "pipelines" were in place, and Evashevski had long since proven that he belonged on any list of college football coaching elite.

Did Evashevski ever regret his choice? Not publicly. He spoke of the stress of coaching, the long hours and the uncertainty of the profession.

"I got tired of seeing some 18-year-old kid running up and down the sideline with my paycheck in his hand," he once jokingly remarked when asked why he got out at such an early age.

Yet there is no question in my mind that he missed the game on the field. Why not? He got out when most men have barely started their head coaching careers, and while in it he dazzled the football establishment with his accomplishments.

I spent a lot of time with Evashevski in those days, traveling to and from games and in the broadcast booth itself (he twice served as my color analyst during the 1960s and later in the 1970s), as well as appearing on our popular "Beat the Bear" TV show. He still had a solid block of support behind the scenes, from powerful Hawkeye backers of the early days down to average fans. I remember one postcard I got during that period said, "It's obvious Iowa needs a quarterback, a halfback and Evashevski back."

What was Evashevski like in those days? That is a question I am still asked. For the most part he was cordial and outgoing on the surface because he was still very much a celebrity wherever we went. I'll never forget one Iowa-Indiana game at Bloomington in the early '70s. None other than Bobby Knight burst into the press box just before game time, grabbed me and said: "My dad was a hero worshipper—he said Tom Harmon was great but that the man who blocked for him, Forest Evashevski, was even greater—and I understand he's working with you today!" I led him to Evy and the two visited enthusiastically for 20 minutes—Knight even agreed to come on with me at halftime.

Knight later paid high tribute to Evashevski and their meeting. During an ESPN basketball telecast in December of 2009, he told play-by-play announcer Brent Musburger, "I have always sought the advice of great coaches not only in basketball, but other sports as well. One of them was Forest Evashevski. He was one of the best. He told me if he were coaching basketball, he would do it just like I do." (Why not? Actually the two were peas out of pod.)

On occasion, Evy would become sullen and preoccupied (the so-called "dark side" emerging), but it was difficult to tell what this all meant because he kept so much inside of him. One thing is certain—he did not lose his sense of humor. At a Wisconsin pre-game press party in Madison, Evashevski acknowledged the appointment of former Badger and L.A. Rams great Elroy "Crazy Legs" Hirsch as athletic director, by noting that "many people felt the program might be tainted by professionalism when Elroy came here. However, after seeing his teams on the field I think those fears are unfounded."

One time during the broadcast of an Iowa-Northwestern game—
a contest marked by sloppy, uninspired play on both sides—the
action was stopped for an injury to a cheerleader, who had been
carried from the field on a stretcher. During the commercial break,
I said: "I guess we've seen about everything but the proverbial dog
on the field." Evy replied: "I think I see twenty-two down there."

Evy's humor extended even to his physical well-being. He told
me he wasn't feeling well. I asked him what was wrong. He
said, "I've got a problem with my plumbing." I asked what he
was doing for it. He said, "I went to the doctor and he stuck a
wire up there." I asked, "What did he find?" Evy said, "Dust."

◇◇◇

Evy loved to razz me. As we were signing off our final broadcast
of the season he said, "Jim, I enjoyed doing these twenty-two
games with you." I said, "Evy, there were just eleven." He said,
"There were the eleven you did and the eleven I saw."

Evy administered the coup de grace of put-downs in the following letter which he sent along with a 75-dollar check (still
un-cashed) to the sponsors (Bill Krause and Gary Kirke) of a
75th birthday party roast they arranged for me at the Glen Oaks
Country Club in 1996.

Evy had a tenuous relationship with many of his coaching
rivals—Woody Hayes among them (an unavoidable clash of
strong personalities)—but one he got along well with was Ara

Forest Evashevski
1482 Bay View Heights Drive
Petoskey, Michigan 49770

aug. 26, 1996

Dear Nancy,

I regret that I am unable to attend Jim's Roast on Sept. 3. I am committed to be in Ohio on that date. However, I am sending $75.00. This is not to go to the scholarship but to Jim directly to repay him for all the checks he has picked up in the last 44 years 1952-1996. The $75.00 equates to $1.70 per year. This is a little more than Jim spent but Jim can keep the surplus because when you love someone who cares about money!

Seriously, give my best to Jim on this Gala occasion. He has been my good friend and always supported me—even on tie

Evy

Parseghian. They had "terms of endearment" for each other. Evy called Ara "the Armenian rag-picker" and Ara called Evy "the Polish junk dealer." When Ara coached at Notre Dame in the late 60s, Moose Krause, the Notre Dame Athletic Director, invited Evy (then Iowa's A.D.), Randy Duncan (my color man) and me to the traditional "Knights of Columbus" Smoker, a huge affair held the night before home games in South Bend. It was an event that normally paid homage to the great winning tradition of the Fighting Irish. That particular night, however, it was the other way around. Parseghian addressed the 1,200 fans with this: "I want you to meet a quarterback and his coach who never lost to Notre Dame—they beat us three straight times, in 1956, 1957 and 1958." Applause rocked the room. It was a moving moment—I could not help but think of Iowa, a football doormat for years, being honored by the mightiest football tradition of them all.

(That 1958 Iowa-Notre Dame game has a special place in my heart. Senator John F. Kennedy, then a presidential candidate nominee, was in the press box and, by the luck of the draw and a little coattail pulling, I got the only halftime interview with him, on WHO. Iowa was leading the Irish by about three touchdowns at the time. "Senator Kennedy," I said, "what do you think of the game?" Then came the perfect reply: "I'm pulling for Iowa...and praying for Notre Dame.")

Evashevski never lost any of his toughness after leaving coaching. (During his turbulent latter days as Athletic Director, the running gag around Iowa City was: "They may fire Evy, but who's going to tell him?"). At an Iowa-Michigan basketball game at old Yost Field House in Ann Arbor, I asked Evy to come on at halftime. When the second half began he discovered he could not get back to his seat because the crowd had jammed in around the edge of the floor. So I invited him to remain with me in our broadcast space at the top of the bleachers. During the first half some big, burly guy in front of me had been throwing things on the floor whenever a call went against Michigan. At the first such instance in the second half, he raised his arm to throw a popcorn box or some such article, and Evy, by reflex action it seemed, reached out with the palm of his hand and gave the man a solid whack across the neck. The man recoiled, then spun around with fists raised, took one look at Evashevski glaring at him, then sat down and did not make a move for the

rest of the game. He looked like a whipped dog. Evy never mentioned the incident later.

During one of our many trips down the highway, sitting there by ourselves, I got up the nerve to question Evy deeply about two things, and in the process give my opinion on both. Why didn't he stay as coach and forget the A.D. job—and why, in the first place, didn't he work to keep Paul Brechler as A.D. since he (Brechler) was a perfect front man for him. Evy never flinched, or admitted he had made a mistake. "I did what I had to do to keep the football program where it was. I had no choice," was his terse answer. In truth, Evashevski was not a compromiser or negotiator. It was not in his nature to do anything but plow straight ahead, regardless of consequences—and win the battle with power, not persuasion. This trait led to his greatness as a coach—and led to his downfall as an administrator.

Some say he overestimated his power, and felt he could come back as coach by public demand. This is probably true to a degree—but the public was never consulted. If it ever had been put to a public vote in the early days of his athletic directorship, I feel he would have won in a landslide—and why not? He had long since proven he was the best coach around.

So, the inevitable question (or questions): Did Evashevski want to come back as coach, and did he try to come back? I give a qualified "yes" in answer to both. There was a time during both the Burns and Nagel regimes in the 1960s when I feel he would have come back in a second had there been a request from the athletic board. There also is not much doubt that plots and plans were being laid behind the scenes to bring him back, both with and without his knowledge and consent. I recall more than one instance when prominent Evashevski backers (on two occasions alumni members of the board itself) appeared at my home to enlist my support for a "Bring Evy Back" movement. Evy and I had numerous phone conversations during this period in which I urged him to declare his candidacy for the job, especially after the firing of Jerry Burns in 1966. (I did an editorial on WHO-TV, saying that the "best candidate for the Iowa job is still in Iowa City.") But Evy refused to "declare" himself publicly. He wanted to be "drafted." The truth is there is no way this could happen. The Athletic Board, in all honesty, was scared to death of him, and they controlled the votes. (Sharm Scheuerman, Iowa Basketball Coach, sided with the board, and later admitted he became "physically ill" when he entered the Field House if he saw Evashevski's car in the parking lot.)

No matter that Evashevski's friends were among the most powerful men in the state, and that he was still regarded as the one person who could return Iowa to national football prominence. Board members were interested mainly in preserving their own well-being and ending the conflict surrounding the Athletic Department—much of which they themselves helped to create. The board, in short, wanted peace at any price.

Much of what happened during the latter part of the Evashevski era has been documented in detail by the print media. Much of it reads like Greek tragedy. Reports of an attempted player revolt and effort to oust the Hawkeye coaching staff, and replace it with Evashevski, received banner headlines. (It did not happen, but there was a black player boycott during Ray Nagel's tenure. One of the leaders was Denny Green, later Minnesota Vikings coach.) It cannot be denied that hearts were broken, spirits were crushed, and turmoil existed in almost every corner. Many of Evashevski's former supporters and co-workers in the Iowa football program turned against him, while others were still staunch backers—depending on how they got along with him personally and whether they were in his "inner circle." There is not much doubt that a "coaching-staff-in-exile" had been formed, waiting for the battle cry to take over (it never came). The conflict reached into the State Legislature, where the Bill Reichardt faction entered the fray against Evashevski. The state was split into warring camps, remnants of which still existed many years later.

The Evashevski era at Iowa came to its official end on May 19, 1970, when the Board of Athletics relieved him of his duties. Bump Elliott was hired to replace him as Athletic Director.

The accomplishments of the Evashevski era stand among the greatest landmarks in Iowa athletic history—a point that was underlined by his induction into the Iowa Hawkeye Hall of Fame, and by the honors accorded him during his two visits to Iowa City in the 1990s.

Finally, whatever may be said negatively of the Evashevski years, to that same degree it must be said positively: He was the right man for the time.

Forest Evashevski died at 11:30 p.m., Friday, October 30, 2009. He was 91 years of age. He succumbed to liver cancer. Memorial services were held on Tuesday, November 3, in Petoskey, Michigan. Among those attending were Iowa Athletic Director Gary Barta, Randy Duncan and Des Moines businessman Bill Krause, who served as a football manager under Evashevski, and who has been a huge Hawkeye backer through the years. It is symbolic and nostalgic, I think, that Evy's passing occurred when Iowa played the same opponent that he played in 1956— Indiana. That was the game in which Evy introduced his famed Wing-T Offense. I remember interviewing him outside of Indiana Stadium before the game. "I don't know what's going to happen," Evy said. "I hope it works."

Indeed, it did work. Iowa beat Indiana that day in 1956, 27-0, and wound up in the Rose Bowl at the end of the season. The 2009 Hawkeyes beat the Hoosiers, 42-24, and went to the Orange Bowl.

POST-SCRIPT: THE REAL EVASHEVSKI—WHO WAS HE?

How well did I know Forest Evashevski? How well did anyone know him? I may have come the closest since I did all of his radio and TV shows, as well as numerous articles and scripts about him, and probably spent more time with him socially and professionally than any other member of the media. Yet, I can't say that I "knew" Evashevski so much as I understood him.

As is the case with many talented, perceptive men who get there "the hard way," Evy set early goals for himself (fame, fortune, a good marriage) and achieved them all. Football gave him fame. He married the lovely Ruth Brown, daughter of industrialist and political leader Prentiss Brown, and there is no question that coaching and activities related to it brought him wealth. He also was an astute investor. (He often said he read the financial section of the paper before the sports page).

Perhaps his greatest talent was in "reading" people and knowing how to handle them. In this sense, he was an actor. (There is nothing wrong with that. Cary Grant once said he spent an entire lifetime trying to be—or play—Cary Grant). At the core of his persona there was an insatiable desire to control—to succeed at almost any cost. Someone once said to me: "Evashevski is using you." I said: "I know it. I'm using him, too."

So, essentially, it was a push. He needed me and I needed him. He was, at the very least, a marketable commodity for us—and

WHO provided strong backing for him. Plus, I will have to admit, I liked him.

How valuable was Evy for us? I will cite just one instance. It is clouded with rumor and hearsay, but I think (since it came from an "inside source") it is probably true. Evy was very good at releasing key information (injuries, lineup changes, etc.) on the Sunday night show I did with him on WHO-TV. This forced the print media, particularly the *Register*, to quote from and credit the show. The story goes that after one especially newsworthy Sunday night, Luther Hill, publisher of the *Register*, came to Leighton Housh, the sports editor, and asked how many people he had working for him. Housh replied "seventeen." How many does WHO have?" came the question. "Zabel and a couple of part-timers," Housh replied. "Then, why do we get beat every week?" came the next question. "Because they own the rights to Evashevski," came the reply. I don't know what was further discussed, but it wasn't long after that that Evy wound up with two regular weekly features in the *Register* ("You-Be-The-Coach" kind of things), for which he was paid.

It is hard to overestimate the importance of Evashevski to the people of Iowa in those days, and around the country too. I did a radio show with him that was cited by the magazine *Texas Monthly* as being one of the most popular radio shows in Houston, a town noted for its many radio talk shows because of drivers being stranded many hours each day on its endless freeways. WHO's big signal blanketed the Lone Star State.

Why, you might ask, did Evashevski become so obsessed with the Iowa job? After all, here was a man who could have made his mark in almost any business or professional endeavor. I think he saw a special challenge in Iowa—a chance to take something from rock bottom to the top, with all the attendant rewards, and gain total control of it. He could not have done this at Michigan, Ohio State or Notre Dame. They were already successful.

In that sense, what we saw was what we got—a brilliant and aggressive man—calculating and designing—who knew how to make things work, but who also brought with him a large bill for the consequences.

Critics claimed Evashevski was "paranoid" or that he was a "psychopath"—a man bent on the destruction of anything he could not control. The late Al Couppee, an early and devout Evashevski supporter who later turned against him, once told me: "Evy could convince you that black was white and white was black. I did stuff for him—like helping to get rid of Brechler (athletic director)—that I had second thoughts about at the time. But I did it, partly because I had blinders on and partly because I thought it would help the Iowa football program. Evy believed that anything he wanted to do, any goal he wanted to reach, was right, regardless of who got hurt. It wasn't just a plot or crazy idea—he really believed it. Years later, after the whole thing was over with and I was in San Diego, he called out of a clear blue sky and invited me to play golf. I was shocked. When we played, he acted as if nothing had ever happened—that everything was business as usual. He didn't apologize. He acted as if we were lifelong friends. I suddenly realized he felt he had done nothing wrong, and actually felt no remorse."

Evy was a driven man, and history has proven that men possessed of and consumed by a total belief in themselves and the righteousness of their cause seldom regret what they have done. They believe they are right. It is the world around them that is wrong.

POST-SCRIPT

Evashevski's wit was demonstrated again at a luncheon honoring Des Moines business leader (and Hawkeye benefactor) Joe Rosenfield on the event of his 90th birthday, April 25, 1994—an occasion so prestigious that the guest list included, among others, Warren Buffet, America's richest man. Upon being introduced to speak, Evashevski said "at a moment like this, I feel a little like Elizabeth Taylor's seventh husband. I know what to do, but I'm not sure I can make it interesting."

Buffet had a few good lines of his own. After tapping the microphone several times with his forefinger before speaking, he said "testing...testing...one-million—two-million—three-million..."

Mrs. Buffet threw a wonderful verbal bouquet at Joe Rosenfield. She said: "In a room full of Ashley Wilkes...you are my Rhett Butler."

POST-SCRIPT #2

Jerry Burns

The most notable single effort to heal the wounds of the Evashevski era came from the man who many believe to be its greatest victim: Jerry Burns. On September 5, 1992, while being honored at the annual Iowa Letterman's Hall of Fame Banquet, Burns paid high tribute to Evashevski with these words: "I had the honor of working with coaching greats like Vince Lombardi and Bud Grant, both of whom coached in Super Bowls, but I'm not sure that the best of them all wasn't Forest

Evashevski. Evy was a genius on the football field. And of all the teams I ever worked with—and this included Super Bowl teams at Minnesota and Green Bay—I really feel the greatest at its level of competition was the 1958 Iowa team. I have never seen a better running back than Willie Fleming—and Randy Duncan has to rank with the best of all quarterbacks."

I served as MC at the banquet, and introduced Randy Duncan for his induction into the Iowa Hall of Fame.

UNSOLVED MYSTERY

Several years ago I did a phone show interview with Bubba Smith, former all-time All-Pro and before that All-American at Michigan State, who was at that time promoting a fitness program he had developed. During a commercial break, I joked with him as to why he did not follow his brother, Willie Ray Smith, to Iowa (Willie Ray stayed there one year, then left). I mentioned knowing that Bubba had been part of the so-called "Beaumont Package"—a highly recruited group of Texas athletes that also included George Webster (voted in 1997 Michigan State's all-time greatest player) and All-American end Gene Washington. Bubba gave me an astounding answer: "The truth is we were recruited by Jerry Burns and wanted to come to Iowa. But before we could get there our visit was cancelled. I never found out why."

I have a strong feeling that had Evashevski been coach, instead of athletic director, these players might well have wound up at Iowa—and Iowa might have been headed for another dynasty.

HAYDEN
MIRACLE MAKER

The importance of Hayden Fry to the Iowa football program cannot be overstated. To put it simply, he saved it.

Iowa football stumbled through twenty years of failure and frustration following the departure of Forest Evashevski and there was some doubt whether it could ever be resurrected. It is a cruel fact of history that schools that hit the skids often stay at the bottom for long periods, football being the numbers game that it is.

It was during this dark era of Hawkeye football that a fan hollered at me as I left the stadium: "Hey Zabel, when I die I want to be buried in the Iowa end zone where no one will step on me!" I told Podolak, "Luckily, there were only two bad decades." Hayden said he took the Iowa job because he felt the Hawkeyes had two of the three things necessary to make a program go—fans and money. "It's up to me," he said, "to supply the third—players."

The first thing Hayden tried to do was bring the warring factions together. He had a two-hour phone conversation with Evashevski. Then he spent time with George Foerstner, CEO of Amana and Raytheon, who controlled the purse strings of financial backing for Iowa football. Foerstner said, "I think I like this guy."

Next, Hayden brought his 16-inch guns to town in the form of an outstanding staff, one of the best, I think, ever assembled. We're talking about guys like Bill Snyder, Barry Alvarez, Kirk Ferentz, Dan McCarney, Carl Jackson, Bill Brashier, Bobby Elliott and later, graduate assistants like Bobby Stoops, Mike Stoops and Bret Bielema. ("I'm proudest of the fact," Hayden said, "that 26 of my assistants went on to become head coaches."). Recruiting was the top priority for this staff, and it paid off with players like Chuck Long, Chuck Hartlieb, Tavian Banks, Tim Dwight,Ronnie Harmon, Quinn Early, Sedrick Shaw, Nick Bell, Larry Station,

COACH HAYDEN FRY
20 YEARS OF EXCELLENCE AT IOWA

Hayden Fry is carried off the field after Iowa defeats Michigan State University, 36-7, on November 21, 1981. The victory propelled Iowa into the Rose Bowl for the first time since 1958.

Dennis Mosley, Jared Devries, Aaron Kampman and Reggie Roby, to mention some of the best.

Trying to pick the greatest games of the Fry regime is tough because there were so many of them. The 1985 win over Michigan, 12-10, has to be high on the list because the Hawkeyes were #1 in the nation, and the Wolverines #2. My personal favorite is the 9-7 victory over Michigan at the Big House in 1981. I like this game because it broke a long and bitter string of Wolverine wins at Ann Arbor and it turned out to be a stepping stone to the Rose Bowl for the Hawkeyes that year. The game had additional meaning for me because Forest Evashevski and Tom Harmon were both in the booth with me. Evy was my color man, and Tom was there with Evy to honor their great Michigan team of 40 years earlier. I asked Evy where he was going as he left the booth, and he said, "Tom and I are going out to find a new coach." As it turned out, Bo kept his job.

My favorite Iowa play that I called was the sensational Hartlieb to Cook pass at Columbus on November 14, 1987, to give the Hawks a 29-27 win and seal the doom of Buckeye coach Earle Bruce. I went slightly crazy on that one. (In fact, State Musicologist Roger Maxwell set my touchdown call to music.

MARC HANSEN

Zabel hits new height

Iowa fans aren't raving about The Play anymore, but they're still talking about The Call.

The Play was the astounding fourth-down, 28-yard touchdown pass that doomed Ohio State a week ago. The Call was the way Jim Zabel, with help from sidekick Ed Podolak, described the miraculous moment over WHO radio in Des Moines.

Zabel, as all true Hawkeye enthusiasts know, has been calling Iowa games since Lee handed off to Grant at Appomattox. When former music teacher Roger Maxwell says the venerable Mr. Z hit a new high last week, he isn't necessarily talking broadcasting excellence.

He's talking vocal range. When Marv Cook caught Chuck Hartlieb's pass at the 9 and barreled over with the winning touchdown, the frenzied Zabel scaled Vienna Boys Choir heights.

I mean he got up there. Explored uncharted territory. A few notes higher and only the canine population would have known the final score.

Maxwell, compliance officer for the state Board of Regents, has been summoned to provide expert witness.

The gentleman's music credentials are impeccable. He has written four books for bands. He has been the conductor of the "Everyone Sings the Messiah" program at the Civic Center. As a hobby, he writes music.

DESPITE HIS impressive background, Maxwell also is a great admirer of Zabel. Saturday's performance, he says, will go down as the day the voice of the Hawkeyes spat in the face of tonal gravity.

Let's pick up the action on the Buckeye 28, fourth and 23.

Printed with permission by the Des Moines Register

He had a soprano from Simpson College sing my part in perfect harmony—"Six seconds to play—Hartlieb fades back—he passes to Cook—he's at the ten—he's at the five—it's a touchdown! It's a touchdown—Iowa wins 29 to 27." The song didn't make the Hit Parade, but it became the first touchdown at the Horseshoe to become an opera.). For the record, it was Bo Pelini, current coach at Nebraska who missed the tackle on Cook at the 5-yard line. That information came from Chris Spielman, when I appeared on his phone show in Columbus.

What was Hayden's favorite game? There were those dramatic wins over Penn State, Ohio State, Michigan and Nebraska, but the one nearest and dearest to his heart was the 55-17 walloping of old rival Fred Akers and the Texas Longhorns in the Freedom Bowl at Anaheim, California, on December 26, 1984. The game was played in a driving rainstorm, but that didn't slow down Chuck Long. The Iowa quarterback set a record with six touchdown passes against the vaunted Longhorns, who had been rated #1 in the nation for five weeks during the season.

I also remember the Freedom Bowl for logistical reasons. I was in Hawaii to broadcast Iowa's appearance in the Rainbow Classic Basketball Tournament. The Hawkeyes lost a 2-point overtime game to Maryland and the late Len Bias on Christmas night. After the game I dashed to the airport to catch a 2:30 a.m. red-eye to Anaheim, 2,500 miles away. After the Freedom Bowl I caught a red-eye back to Honolulu, arriving just in time to broadcast the Hawkeye basketball team in the consolation round of the tournament, which started at noon. Such were the hectic schedules we kept while covering the Hawkeyes in those days.

In 20 years of doing Hayden's pregame radio shows and postgame TV shows I shared many intimate moments with him. He had a running tug-of-war with team doctors over players being sidelined by injury for extended periods. "If you've got a hangnail you don't play," he once complained to me. On another occasion, star running back David Hudson had been sidelined for several weeks with a strained quadricep (upper leg). When I arrived at Hayden's office to do his pregame show, I could tell he was in a testy mood. "The doc called me today," he told me, "and said I've got good news about David Hudson—'he can pedal a bicycle.'" Hayden said, "I told him, 'Good, maybe we can get him a paper route.'"

Another time we were scheduled to tape the Hayden Fry TV show at 10 a.m. Sunday in the East Hall Studio, and Hayden was late which was unusual for him. He finally showed up and explained he was late because he had to take his dog to the vet. "You know how Dobermans are, they want to investigate everything," Hayden said. "Our home is near the reservoir and when he saw an eagle holding a fish in his claws he thought he was King Kong and tried to get the fish away. The eagle was the winner. The dog wound up with 84 stitches."

Going to the Rose Bowl with Hayden in 1981 was a fabulous experience. I emceed the Hawkeye pep rally held at the luxurious Century Plaza Hotel. I called Bill Quinn, the hotel manager, who came from Carroll, Iowa and was a friend. Bill assured me the hotel was ready for a big crowd. "We can accommodate a sit-down dinner for 5,000 people," he said. The problem was that 27,000 fans showed up. They completely overcrowded the lobby, jamming the escalator and the elevators. I led cheers as best I could, going from one party area to another. Some people were even wading in the pool in front of the hotel. Bill Quinn said afterward, "I hired five extra bartenders. I could have used 50."

Hayden was never at a loss for words when it came to handling the actions of boisterous fans. One time during a game against Wisconsin at Madison, there were complaints about Badger fans getting out of line. On his radio show that I did with him, one Hawkeye fan called in and said, "When we came out of the tunnel, some Wisconsin fans were pouring schnapps on us. What should we have done? " Hayden said, "Just put your head back and enjoy it."

Another time we got to talking about Texas chili on the show. I asked Hayden what the difference was between 4-alarm and 5-alarm chili. He said, "5-alarm is where you put the armadillo in live."

One night we took a call from a truck driver who said he was just pulling into Denver and was listening to the show. He had a strong Texas accent! He asked, "Are you the same Hayden Fry who played quarterback for Odessa High School? " Hayden said he was. "This is Gus Johnson," the caller said, "I played fullback on that team. Remember me?" Hayden gave him a big greeting, and said he did indeed remember him. The caller then asked, "Hayden, what are you doing now?" Hayden took it right in stride, and explained he was coaching football at the University of Iowa. "No kidding!" the caller said, "I always knew you was bigger than Odessa. Maybe I'll catch one of your games some time." I told Hayden that fame brings many rewards, some when you least expect them.

Not everyone was happy with Hayden Fry's exclusive arrangement with WHO. On June 17, 1990, the *Cedar Rapids Gazette*

carried a two-column full-page story with this headline: "Mitchell Zaps Fry over Deal with WHO Radio". The article, by Jim Ecker, reads "When (Frosty) Mitchell said 'Fry has always sold his soul to WHO,' he was referring to the Thursday night call-in show, hosted by Jim Zabel, and to the post-game interview conducted for WHO by Phil Haddy, Iowa's assistant sports information director.

"Mitchell thinks Fry deliberately withholds information at his Tuesday press conference for use on Thursday night. And he described the postgame session with Haddy as a 'House Interview'—without substance!"

The truth was that every other coach in the Big 10 had exclusive contracts for radio and television shows so Hayden was no different.

The 1998 season was a bad one for Hayden personally and for Iowa football. The Hawkeyes lost five straight games to end the season, finishing with a 3 and 8 record.

I did Hayden's last TV show as Iowa coach, following the Hawkeyes 49-7 loss to Minnesota on Nov. 21, 1998. He looked very tired at the taping. Actually, he was a sick man. (Prostate cancer, and later bladder cancer which required surgery). After a brief period of disappointment felt by his many fans, his popularity produced a host of banquets and tributes which continue today. He remains one of Iowa's most beloved coaches. "They even named a highway after me," Hayden exclaimed when I talked with him in December, 2009. "Now the fans who tailgate a little too much after the game can leave by the Fryway."

Rick Klatt, Iowa's associate athletic director, also organized a "Fryfest " before the first game in 2009. "It was great," Hayden said, "I loved seeing all of my old friends, and even the ones who weren't so friendly when I was coaching. I guess they think I've improved with age."

Hayden admits he has had to cut back on his activities — "I was on twelve boards of directors," he said. "I've cut those down to three. One I hated to give up was the Hula Bowl in Hawaii. But I told them I had seen all the grass skirts and had drunk all the coconut milk I could take."

Not everything has been that pleasant. National Public Radio called him for an interview. They wanted to talk about his famous pink locker room. "All of a sudden," he said, "they brought in the president of the National Lesbian Society and she started blasting me on the air, telling me how demeaning it was."

"What did you say? " I asked. Hayden said, "I told her, 'Lady, I don't care how badly you had to use the bathroom, I would never let you in my pink locker room.' Then I hung up on her. After that, "National Public Radio called back and I hung up on them also."

Sometimes Hayden's popularity resulted in service above and beyond the call of duty. He attended the funeral for the father of the Stoops brothers, who passed away unexpectedly while coaching a game in Youngstown, Ohio. Mrs. Stoops, the widow, asked Hayden for a favor. Could he raise her husband's body out of the casket and put a Hawkeye jersey on him? Hayden obliged and Coach Stoops was buried in Hawkeye colors.

The search for a new head coach at Iowa took a lot of twists and turns, with the name of Bobby Stoops being most prominently mentioned. But Iowa was up against a deadline because Oklahoma also wanted Stoops. And the Sooners won out. (There were those who swore Stoops really wanted the Iowa job. I interviewed him at half-time of an Arena Football game in Oklahoma City, and asked him that very question. He laughed and said he loved Iowa City and the Hawkeyes, but was happy at Oklahoma. He added, "Iowa has a great coach in Kirk Ferentz."). It is an open secret that Bob Bowlsby's favorite candidate was his buddy at UNI, Terry Allen, who was at Kansas at that time. But he was struggling and quickly fell out of the picture. Next came interviews with former Iowa assistants, including Kirk Ferentz. Gradually, Kirk became the favorite and was hired. So once again he was in familiar territory. Obviously, Kirk was the perfect choice, and he seemed to possess the same ability to come from behind and win the race that Bowlsby himself had. I felt it was a great selection from the beginning. I had gotten to know him very well when he was with Hayden and had done many interviews with him because I have always felt a great offensive line coach is the keystone of a successful coaching staff. Those dramatic wins over Michigan in the 1980s—I always believed Kirk deserved a large share of the credit— so from that standpoint, he is really an extension and continuation of the Hayden Fry days. And that's good enough for me.

KIRK
POWER! PERFORMANCE! PRESTIGE!

Sherlock Holmes said, "When you eliminate the impossible, the improbable becomes the truth." My feeling of improbability for Iowa football started in 1949 when I was watching a Michigan football practice in Ann Arbor. I was making a tour of the Big 10 before my first year of broadcasting Hawkeye football. A guy standing next to me asked where I was from. I said, "Iowa." Then he said very matter-of-factly, "You guys don't belong in the Big 10."

I never forgot that arrogant statement, and hoped that guy was listening and watching in 1956 when Iowa beat Minnesota 7-0, Ohio State 6-0, Notre Dame in a non-conference season-ender 48-8, then on to the Rose Bowl where the Hawks beat Oregon State 35-19. (I know the Michigan guy would say, "Yeah, but what was the one team that beat you in 1956? Its colors are maize and blue." I would respond very calmly but firmly, "Yes, but who went to the Rose Bowl?")

I will have to admit, it was the high point of my sports career at that time, and it remains just as improbable today—except that it has been exceeded by something even more improbable—the Hawkeyes of 2009. Sure, we all knew they would be good—but the way they won games?! Are you kidding?! Nobody could block two field goals in seven seconds, or come from behind to win eight games, or beat Penn State, Michigan State, Iowa State, and Wisconsin on the road in the same season. Nobody does that, do they? If you would have asked me that question in 1959, after two Big 10 championships and two Rose Bowl victories, I would have said, "Of course they do. Iowa does it all the time." We were a cocky bunch back then. We thought anything was possible as long as Evashevski was there. (Evy said, "I teach my players to be gracious winners. Let the other side be good losers."). Little did we realize that

Evashevski would be gone in a year and the Hawkeyes would not win another BCS-class bowl game for half a century.

As I watched and listened to Iowa's dominating 24-14 win over Georgia Tech, with its supposed "unstoppable" triple-option offense, I was transported back to those halcyon days of the 1950s, when the sky was the limit. On that cold Miami night, I had the same feeling.

My "Sound-Off" partner Jon Miller and I both picked Iowa to go 10 and 2, but who could have foreseen Adrian Clayborn's blocked punt against Penn State, or the Stanzi-McNutt touchdown pass against Michigan State with two seconds on the clock, or the last minute heroics against Indiana or the Ramblin' Wreckage Iowa created in the Orange Bowl. Maybe the time has come to accept Iowa's improbable feats as a norm— or as Holmes would say, as the truth. Perfection, sometimes, is impossible to achieve. But don't tell that to Iowa fans, or players.

"In your pursuit of perfection," Vince Lombardi said, "you can achieve excellence."— and that is exactly what Kirk Ferentz has done. His teams exude <u>Power</u>; they have thrilled Hawkeye fans everywhere with brilliant <u>Performances</u>, and they have brought <u>Prestige</u> to Iowa that is recognized across the nation.

A three-time Big 10 Coach of the Year, and winner of the National Coach of the Year Award in 2002, Ferentz is viewed by most as a man of calm demeanor who keeps his emotions under wraps. "He has absolutely no ego," says defensive coordinator Norm Parker, in an article written by Rick Klatt. "He is a joy to work with." But make no mistake, Kirk Ferentz is as tough as a Norm Parker Red-Zone Defense. They used to say of Bud Wilkinson, the great former Oklahoma coach, "He wears velvet gloves, but there are talons underneath."

I did many interviews with Kirk Ferentz during his years with Hayden Fry. Hayden recognized talent in Kirk right away, even though Kirk stretched the facts a bit when he was hired. "He told me a couple of little fibs," Hayden said. "He told me he was 28, when he was really 26, and he said he was offensive line coach at Pittsburgh, when he was really a grad assistant. But when I put him at the blackboard, he was miles ahead of everyone else."

I doubt that there is another coach in the country more admired by his peers than Kirk Ferentz. Bill Parcells, coach of two Super Bowl championship teams, paid a special visit to an Iowa practice at the Orange Bowl. "I have long been an admirer of Coach Ferentz' program," Parcells said. "We're looking for the same kind of reliable, dependable, accountable, smart, tough, disciplined players that your coach recruits."

Recruiting, of course, is the essence of any successful football program, and Ferentz ranks among the best in that department. I have heard it said many times that Kirk gets "his kind of guy and develops him into his kind of player." The record speaks for itself. As of 2010, Iowa had 38 players in the pros, and in a January 2010 playoff victory over Cincinnati, former Hawkeye Shonn Greene rushed for 135 yards for the New York Jets. The next week he got 125 yards against San Diego. (Just think of the possibilities if he had played his senior year at Iowa. But give him credit. Shonn did come back to serve as honorary captain, and gave Adrian Clayborn, national defensive player of the year, the advice to stay at Iowa for his senior year. Adrian heeded the advice.)

Ferentz' qualities of loyalty and longevity have served him well in recruiting and coaching. His players are as passionately loyal to each other as Ferentz is to them. The same with his coaches. The chemistry on the Iowa squad is evident in their intensity of play. Iowa fans and contributors are equally exuberant about Ferentz. Dale Howard tells of the trip to New York for the Hall of Fame ceremony honoring Iowa linebacker Larry Station. "Kirk couldn't do enough for us," Howard said. "He gave up his reservation at the Waldorf so that he could stay at our hotel and spend more time with us."

TV football analyst Matt Millen said of Ferentz, "He's a great guy, and he runs the best football program in the country." ESPN's Mark May picked Iowa to beat Ohio State. Afterward, he said, "The Hawkeyes played a great game. To think you could come into the Horseshoe before one-hundred-five thousand people with a freshman quarterback who had never started a Big 10 game, and you carry Ohio State into overtime—it's incredible. Great coaching job and great play by Vandenberg."

Considering that Iowa is the smallest state in the Big 10 (Chicago has more cars than Iowa has people), it makes Ferentz' accomplishments all the more amazing. "Kirk Ferentz doesn't get many 5-star or 4-star recruits," TV analyst Bob Griese says, "but he gets his kind of recruits and molds them into his kind of players. He is very loyal to his players and coaches, and I think that has paid off."

The much-maligned Big 10 (Iowa was the only Big 10 bowl winner in 2008) appears to have made a comeback with 2009-10 bowl wins by Iowa, Ohio State, Penn State and Wisconsin, and near misses by three other Big 10 teams. One sSouthern sports columnist put it this way, "Speed seems to be working its way north," referring to the oft-stated disparity in that commodity between the Big 10 and the SEC and Pac-10. (In recent years, Iowa has scored bowl wins over such Southern powerhouses as LSU, Florida, South Carolina and, of course, Georgia Tech.) If anything, the Big 10 appears to be on the threshold of a renaissance. Competition within the conference the next few years should be fierce. Wisconsin's Bret Bielema issued a challenge of sorts after the Badgers' bowl victory over Miami; "The teams that beat us last year are on our schedule in 2010," he said, "and we can't wait."

I have a feeling the Hawkeyes will be ready. That's not improbable. It's the truth.

I couldn't have covered a single game without Mother Podolak's chili!
Photo printed with permission by the Des Moines Register

THE A.D.S
BRECHLER, BOWLSBY, & BEYOND

There was a roast for Bob Bowlsby which I attended, shortly before he left UNI for Iowa. After a night of taunts, jabs and general frivolity, his banker came to the microphone and said "Bob, when you were named Uni-Dome manager, you were the second choice. When you got the athletic directorship at UNI, you were also the second choice. And when you got the Iowa job you were the third choice!" Then after a long pause, he said "Are you sure your wife hasn't been married before?"

The humor of the moment belied the truth that it signified. Namely, that Bowlsby has often appeared out of the race, but he has rarely lost it. (Even the Stanford job reportedly came to Bowlsby more by default than by design. The Stanford search committee supposedly called him for advice and he decided, and they realized, that he himself was the man for the job. In short, the timing was right for both sides.)

Bowlsby represented a new breed of athletic director when he came to Iowa. In the past, most schools had given the job to an ex-coach or former player who could meet and greet the wealthy alums. Bowlsby was a business manager and CEO—and, most important of all, a project planner and fund-raiser. Iowa had just four athletic directors over a 55-year span: Paul Brechler, Forest Evashevski, Bump Elliott, and Bob Bowlsby.

Bob Bowlsby with BJ Armstrong

I worked with all of them. How would I rate them? Briefly, this way:

MOST POPULAR—Bump Elliott. A legendary athlete himself, he hired five of Iowa's greatest coaches—Hayden Fry, Lute Olson, Dan Gable, Vivian Stringer, and Tom Davis. Bump was a "people person." He had time for everyone, and would always listen to your problems.

MOST EFFICIENT—Bob Bowlsby. He hired Kirk Ferentz and carried out the massive Kinnick Stadium renovation. But there were lingering problems in the basketball ranks and general handling of coaches. Sometimes called "The Teflon Man" because he was mainly concerned with the big picture (over individual problems), still it must be said that he stood by Kirk Ferentz in his troubled early years, and he made Kinnick Stadium one of the true showplaces in the Big 10. (A few purely personal observations: I always felt that Steve Alford was a better coach than his record at Iowa showed, but he was in the wrong place. He should have been at Indiana. He was worshipped in the Hoosier State for both his legendary high school and Indiana University heroics. He was not comfortable at Iowa, and his personality reflected that unease. He also had to battle a number of off-the-court problems, such as the Pierre Pierce affair. As for his coaching ability, check his record at New Mexico since he left Iowa—you might be surprised. Credit Alford for taking top-notch assistant coach Craig Neal with him. Tom Davis was also a thorny case for Bowlsby. He was personally popular and was regarded as one of the nation's top coaches. He led the Hawkeyes to the NCAA or NIT tournaments in all but two of the 14 years he was at Iowa. I respected him as much as any coach I have ever worked with, and considered him a personal friend. I traveled to Europe, and both Korea and China with the Iowa team.

What went wrong? Why was he dismissed, especially after a 20-win season and two NCAA tournament victories? The blunt truth: it was recruiting. Roy Williams rode into Iowa and staged the great talent robbery—taking Raef LaFrentz, Nick Collison, and Kirk Hinrich back to Kansas with him. He compounded that recruiting hat trick by later grabbing Harrison Barnes for North Carolina. True, Tom Davis got Ricky Davis. If he could have gotten two of the other three, particularly LaFrentz, I feel he might still be at Iowa today, and further, might be succeeded by his son, Keno, when he retired. I know this scenario may be chalked up to the ruminations of an idle mind, but I feel it veers pretty close to the logical progression of "what might have been".

MOST UNDERRATED—Paul Brechler. Part of a distant past, and largely remembered for his tumultuous relationship with Forest Evashevski, but just think of it—his reign produced the greatest record in Hawkeye history. In one four-year span, Iowa won two Rose Bowl games and went to  back-to-back Final Fours, playing San Francisco for the NCAA championship in 1956. Brechler was widely respected in athletic circles. CBS Sports President Bill McPhail offered him a top position at the network but Brechler turned it down. (I know this because he showed me the correspondence).

MOST ENIGMATIC—Forest Evashevski. Revered as a football coach, his blunt, hard-nosed style made him difficult to evaluate as an administrator. He hired Ralph Miller, one of the nation's premier basketball coaches, but Hawkeye football teams managed only one winning season during his tenure, and there seemed to be constant turmoil behind the scenes in the athletic department. Bubbling beneath the surface was the feeling that Evashevski really wanted to coach—and many fans shared that view.

GARY BARTA—Too early to make a final assessment, but all signs point to a bright future. Why not? Football already is flying high, wrestling is a dynasty, Women's Basketball is on the upswing, and the Athletic Building Program is flourishing, spearheaded by the fund-raising prowess of Barta and Mark Jennings.

Now it's up to new Basketball Coach Fran McCaffery to provide the next pillar of success in Hawkeye Athletics. There is every reason to believe he can recruit and coach and fill the seats of Carver-Hawkeye like it was in the "Glory Days." That would bring a resounding vote of confidence for Barta, who I feel handled the selection process quickly and with a consensus of positive opinion by involving former players like Bobby Hansen, Kenyon Murray and Jess Settles in the hiring procedure and in the first press conference with Coach McCaffery.

The failure of Todd Lickliter, I think, will baffle us for years to come. Here was a man who had been National Coach of the Year, who led his Butler team to the Sweet 16 (and perhaps can claim some credit for Butler's breathtaking performance in the Final Four in 2010), then he came to Iowa and it was all downhill. Barta knows you can be deceived by a resume. This time, he feels certain he made the right choice.

I'm an optimist. I predict McCaffery will make an immediate impact—first on fans on the I-Club circuit, then on victories (from 10 to 18?) and on attendance (from 5,000 to 10,000?). After that, open up those Golden NCAA Gates!! (I can hear the cries now: "Zabel's crazy again." No, I'm not. I believe in this guy. He is exciting and he plays exciting basketball. As for the other predications, I am long on hope. But my car is double-parked and the motor is running.)

ICONS: ROCK, ZUP, FRITZ, BO, WOODY, DUFFY & MORE

Rockne and Zuppke. When it comes to coaching legends, it's hard to top these two. Both were innovators, motivators and headline-makers. Zuppke coached the incomparable Red Grange at Illinois and won four national championships; Rockne built a football dynasty around the "Four Horsemen" at Notre Dame. Yet, as is true with many contemporary coaching rivals, they envied and resented each other. In Zuppke's case, the feelings were stronger since he outlived Rockne by some 30 years—Rockne having died in a plane crash in 1931, an event that carried as much impact and drama at that time as the death of a president.

It was with these facts as background that I interviewed Zuppke at his Champaign (Illinois) apartment in fall of 1949, as part of a pre-season Big 10 tour—my first year of broadcasting football for WHO.

Zuppke was sipping a bourbon as I entered his apartment. "My doctor told me a couple of drinks a day will help my heart," he said with that clipped German accent that gave him the air of a Prussian general. Then came a series of remarkable responses from the crusty old coach. I asked him about Fritz Crisler's great 1947 Michigan team which won the national championship with a dazzling display of single-wing football.

"Hell, I used that stuff 35 years ago at Oak Park High School," Zuppke snorted. "Crisler didn't invent the spinning-fullback, buck-lateral series—I did!" He then gave an elaborate demonstration of the offenses run by his Oak Park High School team years before, darting and hopping about the room as he spoke.

On the subject of Rockne, he was even more vehement. He was obviously embittered by the Notre Dame coach's continuing legendary status, decades after his death.

"How great was Rockne?" I asked.

"Let's say he died at a very opportune time!" Zupke snapped.

What Zuppke may have meant (although I am not sure) was that Rockne—by having been snatched away at the very zenith of his fame—did not live to experience the slow, painful decline that is the fate of many coaches if they stay on the job long enough. Zuppke resented this.

When I asked him if he ever went to Illinois football practice (now that Ray Eliot was coach), he said bluntly "No! I might say something!"

Concluding the interview, I could not resist asking Zuppke for his description of a sports announcer, since I was just starting my career. His answer remains to this day perhaps the best I have heard: "A sports announcer is a controlled scatterbrain."

Zuppke's successor at Illinois, Ray Eliot, was a wit and raconteur in his own right. I asked him one time about a game (against Colgate, I think) in which the highly favored Illini barely made it through the first half, and then exploded for 40 points in the second half.

"What did you tell those guys at halftime?" I asked.

"Nothing!" Eliot replied. "I just sat and stared at them!" Then, as an afterthought: "Wait a minute. I did say one thing. When they were leaving the locker room, I said "Good luck, girls."

Fritz Crisler was one of the legitimate geniuses of college football. He created winning programs at Princeton and Minnesota—and a dynasty at Michigan. At Princeton, he communed with noted writer F. Scott Fitzgerald, who would get drunk on Friday night and call him with plays for next day's game. Crisler was dapper and charming, as well as a great coach. He was known to have an eye for the "well-turned ankle" as well. At the 1948 Rose Bowl he delegated preparations part of the time to assistant Bennie Oosterbaan. One day, at a particularly sluggish practice, Crisler drove up in a yellow convertible, decked out in a double-breasted blue blazer, with a young starlet at this side. "The trouble with you guys," he shouted, "is you've gone Hollywood!"

When Crisler was athletic director, I had him on at halftime of an Iowa-Michigan game in Ann Arbor. "Would the great old Michigan single-wing work today?" I asked him. "Yes!" he replied emphatically. "If we could get the linebackers to stand still." Penetrating defenses, of course, killed the single-wing, with its intricate and slow developing plays.

Michigan beat Stanford 49–0 in the first Rose Bowl, back in 1908. The Wolverines defeated USC by the same score in the 1948 Rose Bowl. I asked Bump Elliott what Crisler said to them after the latter game. "He said, 'you guys haven't improved one bit!'"

Duffy Daugherty was renowned for his wit and story-telling prowess as coach at Michigan State. He was also quick to deflect the media's pointed questions. I covered his great 1965 team in the Rose Bowl—a squad that boasted such All-Americans as Bubba Smith, George Webster, Gene Washington and Clinton Jones. One day at the regular post-practice briefing at the Huntington-Sheraton Hotel press room, a Los Angeles writer asked, "Your team has looked sort of ragged in practice, coach—is there any dissension on the squad?"

Daugherty thought about it for a minute, then answered: "You know, I was worried about that, too. So I called a meeting of the offensive starters last night and told them—'I've been hearing reports that some of you guys think you're bigger than the team.' So I had them take a secret ballot as to who was more important, the line or the backfield!" Daugherty paused. Then said, almost as an afterthought, "The line won, 7 to 4."

Duffy's favorite banquet story had to do with the demise of Paddy O'Flarhety. Paddy worked in the Guinness Stout Brewery in Dublin. One day he got too close to the 15,000 gallon main vat, fell in and drowned. The manager and his assistant had the unhappy task of informing the widow O'Flarhety of the tragedy.

"Poor Paddy," she sobbed. "Couldn't swim a stroke. Never had a chance, did he?"

"Well, as a matter of fact he did," the manager replied—"the three times he got out to pee."

Bo Schembechler and Hayden Fry had a give-and-take relationship that started when Bo discovered the famous "pink" locker room in Kinnick Stadium, and sent his managers out to get white butcher paper to cover the walls. Hayden held his own with Bo on the field in the early 1980's, winning three of five, including the 9-7 upset in 1981 that sent the Hawkeyes to the Rose Bowl. In 1984 came the 26-0 Iowa victory that handed Bo his worst Big 10 loss ever. Then there was the fabled 1985 game.

Who can forget 1985? There was more media hype than any game in Iowa history. And with good reason. The Hawkeyes were rated #1 in the nation, and the Wolverines were #2. Hayden thought he would relieve the pre-game tension by resorting to a little trickery. So, in the warm-ups, right in front of the Michigan bench, he had one of his tackles fill in at center and snap the ball to the kicker. The ball sailed 5 feet over the punter's head. "My God, are you going to use that guy during the game?!" Bo asked emphatically. Hayden answered coolly: "We don't intend to have to punt." (Iowa won the game 12-10 to stay #1 in the nation).

Bo was one of the "stars" of the acclaimed film "The Big Chill." The story took place during a Michigan football weekend, and Bo was on-screen (TV, that is) almost as much as Glen Close. I asked Bo what he got paid. He said: "Not a dime. All I was trying to do was win a football game and I guess that wasn't part of their storyline."

Woody Hayes was colorful, volatile and loved to talk. My spotter at Ohio State alluded to that one time when he said: "We've got the real cowboy team this year. Hopalong Cassady, the Cisco Kid (Fullback Galen Cisco) and Gabby Hayes."

Cassady won the Heisman at Ohio State and cut quite a figure himself around Columbus. During the course of a pretty exuberant night of partying with Iowa fans that were in the same hotel with Cassady, the former Buckeye star agreed to come on with me at halftime the next day. On the way to the game, my color man, Randy Duncan, said, "I saw Cassady last night. There's no way he's going to make it today." I told Randy, "I've got a theory about old jocks. They can smell a microphone 10 miles away." Sure enough, the door creaked open at halftime, and there was Cassady, a little the worse for wear, but not of memory—he could remember every touchdown he ever scored.

I later told that story to Paul Giel, former great Minnesota player and later athletic director—and asked him to come on with me at halftime in Minneapolis. At the end of the evening, when we left the press party, I again reminded Giel of the halftime interview the next day, and he said: "I'll be there. Don't forget—us old jocks can smell a mike 10 miles away!"

Vic Janowicz, another Buckeye Heisman winner, played in the most lopsided Iowa-Ohio State game of all time—the 83-21

debacle at Columbus in 1950. Wes Fesler was coach (Woody came in the next year) and he never called off the dogs. Janowicz scored six touchdowns and kicked 10 extra points—a Big 10 record. Exactly 37 years later (November 14, 1987), I had Janowicz on at halftime, along with Athletic Director Rick Bay and OSU President Ed Jennings. All stated emphatically that Coach Earle Bruce's job "was safe". That's when Ohio State was leading. The end of the game provided the most spectacular single play in the history of the series (and, I think, of Iowa football generally) when Chuck Hartlieb hit Marv Cook with the winning touchdown, with six seconds to play. The final was 29-27, and Earle Bruce was fired the following Tuesday.

Some 10 years later, when Bruce was coaching the St. Louis Stampede of the Arena Football League, I was doing the Iowa Barnstormers game against him at the Kiel Center in St. Louis. I came up to Earle with my tape recorder and said: "Coach, you always manage to land on your feet. From Iowa State to Ohio State, to UNI, then Colorado State and now here." Earle got that fiery look in his eye he was famous for, poked his forefinger into my chest and said: "Yes, and I would still be at Ohio State if it wasn't for that damn Iowa game!"

Vic Janowicz' most famous game at Ohio State, and probably the one that won him the Heisman in 1950, was not the 83-21 pounding of Iowa. It was the legendary season-ending meeting with Michigan, still referred to simply as "The Snow Bowl". It was a classic battle of two great punters—Janowicz and Chuck Ortman of Michigan—played in a driving 12-inch snowstorm. For the record, Janowicz punted 21 times for a grand total of 685 yards. But his greatest accomplishment came in the closing minutes of the game, with the goal posts barely visible through the swirling snow, when he kicked a 27-yard field goal—giving Ohio State a 3-0 victory.

Talking about Columbus, on one of my trips there in the early
'50s, Jack Buck (later of St. Louis Cardinals fame) was doing
play-by-play for the Buckeyes, and was working in the booth
next to me. We were in a state of panic before the game because
whoever made out the schedule apparently forgot that Columbus was on Eastern Time, so we started the broadcast one-hour
early. I quickly raced over and I got Buck and he agreed to help
me fill the time. The two of us talked for 60 minutes, right up till
game time. Years later, when Buck had a long rain-delay during
a Cardinal broadcast, he said: "Where is Jim Zabel when I need
him? He owes me one." He then explained the Ohio State incident years before.

Back in 1970, Buck's station in St. Louis—KMOX—flew me
down for an interview. Harry Caray had left for Chicago,
so they wanted me for sports as well as general interest talk
shows. Buck had recommended me to Bob Hyland, the general manager and one of the giants of AM radio broadcasting.
I couldn't make up my mind. The offer was very enticing, and
Hyland was a powerhouse of persuasion. He flew me down to
St. Louis two more times, and on the final visit sent me over
to see Buck in his penthouse apartment overlooking the Mississippi River. There was a baby crawling on the floor (from
Jack's second family). Jack urged me to take the job. I almost
did—largely because of Jack—but for various considerations,
including a young family my own, I turned it down. Years later,
while speaking in St. Louis to an Iowa gathering, Jack invited
me to sit in for two innings of his Cardinal broadcast. During
our on-air conversation, Jack pointed to the young man working with him, and said, "Remember that baby on the floor when
you came to visit me in 1970? That's him." It was Joe Buck, now
a famous broadcaster in his own right.

One of my truly great thrills as an interviewer was when I had Bob Feller and Ted Williams on opposite sides of the microphone for one hour—arguably the greatest pitcher and greatest hitter in major league history. (Williams was in town to help Feller with his Van Meter museum, which we were promoting). Both could remember every single at-bat against each other. In the course of a lengthy and definitive question and answer session, I asked Feller how much Williams would be making if he were playing today.

"At least $10-million a year," Feller said, "and worth every dime of it."

I told that story to Ed Podolak, and about two weeks later he had Mickey Mantle in his golf tournament in Aspen, and he asked him, "Mickey, if you were playing today, how much would you be making?" Mantle thought for a moment, and then said "About $600-thousand." Podolak was shocked. "Only 600-thousand?" he said. Mantle replied: "Yes, but I'm 64 years old."

With Ed Podolak at the Rose Bowl

With the emphasis on the Home Run Derby this past year, I recall an interview I did with Gil Hodges of the Dodgers, the year that he led the majors with 34 home runs by the All-Star break. I caught up with him when they were playing the Cubs in Chicago, and asked him: "Do you have any idea you're going to hit a home run when you head to the ball park?"

"None at all," he answered. "About two weeks ago I didn't feel good, I had a headache and I'd had an argument with my wife that morning. But I went to the ball park—and that day I hit three home runs."

I called the auto races at the fairgrounds for 13 years, and also did special races at 12 other Iowa tracks, including Knoxville, Chariton, Oskaloosa, Boone, Cedar Rapids and Mason City. I was a big fan of dirt track racing, much as Reagan was back in his day, when Barney Oldfield was the star. Today the Iowa Speedway at Newton ranks among the major tracks in the nation, and Knoxville and Boone are also going strong with their annual championship races.

Interviewing Richard Petty

Casey Stengel could mangle the English language—but he could also be very succinct. I did an interview with him at the old Polo Grounds in New York, when he was managing the hapless Mets (before the construction of Shea Stadium). "What can you tell young ball players about their chances with the Mets?" I asked Stengel. He thought for a moment, and then said: "Tell them their chances are good, because we are not established at nine positions."

◇◇◇

Former Big 10 Commissioner Wayne Duke tells of the time he was meeting with Neal Pilson, head of CBS Sports, in New York. Pilson called a popular Italian restaurant for reservations—a restaurant that had been on the front pages recently because of the assassination of Mafia leader Paul Castiglione, which took place in front of the establishment. Pilson said into the phone: "I'd like reservations for two—in the non-shooting section."

UI dormitory residents honor WHO 'radio god' — Jim Zabel

By Rochelle Bozman
Staff Writer

Get out the party hats and blow up the balloons — today is Jim Zabel Day.

Although the day has not been officially approved by the UI Student Senate, UI Student Senate President Tim Dickson, who said he is a "card carrying member" of the Jim Zabel Fan Club, said he plans to go along with the measure and that it should be approved during the senate meeting tonight.

The third-annual dinner for the WHO radio sports reporter from Des Moines will be at 5 p.m. in the North Dining Room in Currier Residence Hall.

Zabel, who has announced Hawkeye basketball games for more than 30 years, replaced Ronald Reagan as the permanent WHO sports announcer after Reagan left for Hollywood, Calif.

"THE VOICE of the Hawkeyes" returned from a short vacation in Phoenix, Ariz., late Wednesday — just in time for the banquet.

"I love it," Zabel said. "I think it's great. It's higher education at its best. We even plan to take a vote to help Lute Olson pick his starting ,line-up for the next two games."

The tradition of the day came from the UI residents of the dormitories, Dickson said, and the senate has gone with the idea for the last two years.

Rick Link, the Currier resident assistant in charge of the day, said Bob Hogue, KWWL sports broadcaster, Maury White, Des Moines Register and Tribune sportswriter and Sharm Scheurman, color commentator for the Iowa Television Network, will be present to "roast" Zabel.

Frosty Mitchell was also scheduled to make an appearance at the dorm dinner, but he "had to cancel out because he had to do some work for the governor," Link said.

"It's an evening to honor Jim Zabel because he has such a broadcasting aura that we were just naturally drawn toward him," Link said. "We consider him a radio god and a media idol."

This quote also appeared in The Daily Iowan's 1981 Jim Zabel Day story. When this was pointed out to Link he said, "Yeah, I know, but I couldn't think of anything better."

MISCUES: (NOBODY'S PERFECT)

Al Couppee—"Paul Hornung will play today with two injured thumbs—one on each hand."

Jim Zabel—"Dusty Rice gets into Michigan's defensive secretary."

Bob Brooks—"They're lining up dog fashion."

Anonymous TV Announcer—"It's the triple-crown of horse raping."

It was a gorgeous day in West Lafayette, and I began my broadcast of the Iowa-Purdue game with a lavish description of the scenery surrounding Ross-Ade Stadium. "And over there," I said, "is Mackey Arena, where the Boilermakers play their basketball games." "Named after Red Mackey," my color analyst Forest Evashevski said, "one of the great men in athletics." "I know," I replied. "I talked to him last night at the press party." "That's amazing," Evy said in a matter-of-fact way, "since he died twelve years ago." A slight case of mistaken identity. It was assistant coach Bernie Crimmins I had talked with, and so far he doesn't have any buildings named after him.

Tom Davis loves this one. I was traveling with the Iowa basketball team to Switzerland and Italy. The team had a dinner cruise on Lake Como, and the next day they were scheduled to go to Venice. They enticed me to get on the microphone during the cruise for a few humorous observations that night. I wound up with a reference to the next day's trip. I said, "I used to know a street walker in Venice, but she drowned." The next day on the team bus, travel director John Streif got on the microphone to tell my story. He was a "straight arrow" kind of guy who thought "street walker" was a bit off-color, so he said, "Jim

My buddy Al Couppee one of the Famous "Ironmen"

Zabel used to have a girlfriend in Venice, but she drowned."
Couldn't save the joke or the girl.

We were talking about Iowa's greatest football victories on
"Sound-Off", and the dramatic 10-7 win over Nebraska in 1981
was one of our top choices. Then someone called and wanted
to know who scored the points in that game. I volunteered
to answer since I did the broadcast. "Roger Craig scored the
touchdown for Nebraska," I said, "and Eddie Phillips scored
the T.D. for Iowa. Then Tommy Nichol kicked the game winning field goal for the Hawkeyes." The switchboard lit up. A
woman on the other end of the line said, "You're wrong! It
was Lon Olejniczak who kicked that field goal." I asked, "How
do you know?" She said, "Because I'm his mother." Then it
came back to me. Lon Olejniczak broke his leg later on, and
Tommy Nichol was the field goal kicker for the rest of the season. I learned something else. You may think you are right, but
mothers are never wrong.

TOUCHDOWNS, INC.
ARENABALL REVIVAL

One of Kurt Warner's most memorable passes, aside from those thrown in Super Bowls, occurred in a building called The Pyramid on the banks of the Mississippi in Memphis, Tennessee. With triple zeros showing on the scoreboard clock, Warner aimed a 40-yard laser at the outstretched hands of Chris Spencer in the end zone. The Iowa Barnstormers came from behind to beat Memphis and headed to the Arena League playoffs.

The game was typical of the kind of last-minute heroics we grew to expect in arena football.

I first encountered arena football when league founder Jim Foster called me from Rockford, Illinois, in 1991 and asked me to do an exhibition game there. I couldn't do it because of a schedule conflict, but two years later, in 1993, I did my first arena game in Des Moines. It was called "The Rumble Under the Roof," and it pitted Cleveland against Arizona at Vets Auditorium. Later that same year I broadcast the first and only Arena All-Star Game for flood relief. Foster brought the Barnstormers to Des Moines in 1994. I became the team's announcer and started a seven-year run filled with spectacular performances, high voltage finishes and upsets galore.

Arena football has a totally different rhythm than 11-man football. Broadcasting the 8-man game, with its forward motion on every play, all of it taking place on a 50-yard field, is more like doing basketball. But it is still blocking and tackling—and lots of passing. I liked it because it was fast, and the games were half as long as college games because the clock runs all the time. I liked it also because some of the players were guys I had covered at Iowa—Carlos James, Larry Blue, Rodney Filer, and Tim Dodge.

It was also great rubbing elbows with the owners like Bruce Heerema of Pella (who once played for the Bears) and Dick Jacobson of Des Moines. "Jake," as we called him has given millions to Iowa, Iowa State, Drake and Grandview. He has athletic buildings named after him at both Iowa and Iowa State. "Yet," he confided to me in 2009, "I think I had my most fun following the Barnstormers." He made all the road trips and was a big booster for the game. We traveled to places like Houston, Louisville, Milwaukee, Albany, Hartford, New York City, Providence, St. Louis, Orlando, Tampa, Memphis, Nashville, San Jose, Anaheim, and Oklahoma City.

Kurt Warner

Kurt Warner was the star of the show from the beginning. His "Rags to Riches" story is well known, but it was his play on the field, as well as his life off the field that set him apart. He had an arm like a rocket-launcher, the eye of an Olympic marksman, and the ability to read defenses with split-second speed—all of which served him well later in the NFL. I interviewed Kurt dozens of times, and had him on my "Beat the Bear" television show as well. He was always cordial, intelligent and informative, and left you with the feeling that great things were ahead for him. His wife Brenda was always with him. She had a strong will of her own, but together you could tell they were perfectly matched. They were, and are, a team—living an inspirational life with their seven children.

Why didn't the original Barnstormers succeed in Des Moines? Quite simply, they priced themselves out of the market. With an 11,000 seat arena, there was no way to cover the mounting costs of player salaries and daily operating expenses. TV plans failed to materialize, and investors were hard to find, especially in the economy of the time. While Arena 1 was dying, Arena 2 was thriving.

The Barnstormers made a resounding comeback as an Arena 2 team in 2008 and 2009, under the ownership of Jeff Lamberti and the solid coaching of veteran John Gregory. Iowa ranks right near the top in attendance, and many league officials think Wells Fargo Arena is the best venue in all of arena football. Now that the league has reorganized, and more realistic financial parameters are in place, I think arena football faces a bright future, and look for the Iowa Barnstormers to be among the best. But don't be late when you go to a game—you could miss three touchdowns.

P.S. Kurt Warner was the star of the evening once again on May 21, 2010, when he became the first former player inducted into the Iowa Barnstormer Hall of Fame.

With owner Jeff Lamberti presiding, his #13 jersey was unfurled from the ceiling of Wells Fargo Arena at halftime. Kurt actually did double duty that night. He served as analyst on the NFL Network telecast of the game. He worked with another Iowa native, Paul Burmeister, former Hawkeye quarterback, who did the play-by-play. Unfortunately, the Barnstormers lost to the Arizona Rattlers, 52-48.

The Barnstormer ownership presented Kurt and Brenda Warner with a check for $50,000 for their charity, the funds coming from a luncheon in Kurt's honor.

Jim Zabel and Gary Fletcher: Voices of the Barnstormers

PENS & SWORDS
THE MEDIA

Sportswriter Jim Murray said of my colleague (and best friend) Ed Podolak, in a *Los Angeles Times* column he did after Eddie's record-breaking performance in the 1971 NFL playoff game with Miami, "If Ed Podolak was a waiter in a gourmet restaurant, his customers would walk out on him because he is too slow. But scouting reports say 'can gain yards on the Russian Army.' "

That single paragraph defines Ed, and also Murray.

Eddie, of course, held the Iowa single-game rushing record for close to 30 years (until Tavian Banks broke it in 1997), and he still holds the NFL single-game playoff record of 350 all-purpose yards, which I doubt will ever be broken.

Murray, who died in August, 1998, was simply the best sportswriter ever. All of the great ones, from Grantland Rice to Red Smith to Bob Considine, left their memorable words and phrases, their dramatic description of the major sports events of our time, but none could match the wit and intellect of Jim Murray.

Who else would say in his lead to the Indy 500: "Gentlemen, start your coffins."

Or at the 1961 World Series—NYY vs. Cincy: "The reason Cincinnati's freeways are not finished is that it was Kentucky's year to use the cement mixer."

Or in describing Michigan State's mammoth 1966 Rose Bowl team: "They're just like any other college football team. They pull their pants on one hoof at a time."

Or on the baseball strike: "If you are in a non-essential business, don't ever let anyone know."

Murray was at his best in describing cities: "San Francisco isn't a city—it's a cocktail party. If you drained the bay, you'd find an olive at the bottom." Two-word description of Chicago in winter time: "Lenin's Tomb." Los Angeles was, at various times, "Norma Desmond" (faded star of "Sunset Boulevard") and "a suburb in search of a city".

Murray is the only writer I know who could make a column (a highly humorous one) out of a routine press release. When it was announced that Yale would appear in the L.A. Classic Holiday Basketball Tournament, Murray wrote, with mock indignation: "What!? Yale in the Los Angeles Classic at Christmas time? They should be back in New Haven delivering plum pudding to the poor..."...and so on, making a case that Yale should be striving for loftier pursuits during the holiday season.

I met Murray firsthand at the 1968 Rose Bowl, in the press room of the Huntington Sheraton, as Indiana was preparing to face USC on New Year's Day. All week long, Murray had been writing things like "Indiana better spend its time practicing kickoff returns because that's all they'll be doing in the Rose Bowl."

That particular day, Murray had written something like "back in 1926, when Hoagy Carmichael was composing the lyrics to 'Stardust' in the basement of his fraternity house on the Indiana campus in Bloomington..."

"How did you know that?" I asked Murray as I started my tape recorder. "Back in 1952," Murray said matter-of-factly, "I was working for *Time* Magazine, and they assigned me to do a cover story on Carmichael. Just as I finished it the Korean War broke out, so *Time* put a general on the cover, and my Carmichael story wound up on the cutting room floor."

I remarked how amazing it was that he could jump so easily from a celebrity cover story to sports writing, and he explained it this way: "What I really am is a 'wordsmith'. I love to put words together, regardless of the topic. Sports lends itself to this better than anything else."

My greatest accomplishment that day, as I recall, was getting Murray and Indiana Coach John Pont on the same tape, despite Murray's persistent ridiculing of the Hoosiers. The reason was Murray's unswerving friendliness, verging on humility. When you met him in person, he was impossible to dislike. (Incidentally, Indiana had nothing to be ashamed of in the Rose Bowl. The Hoosiers lost 14-3 to O.J. Simpson's Southern Cal Trojans, in a game that was close all the way).

I even forgave Murray his jabs against the Iowa Hawkeyes, when they lost 45-28 to UCLA in the 1986 Rose Bowl. "You are going to have to start covering your eyes when these guys come to town in the family Winnebago with their pacemakers and the chicken salad," Murray wrote. "These people are the salt of the earth. They feed the world. They just can't play football."

In 1991, when Iowa lost to Washington, 46-34, in the Rose Bowl, a kinder, gentler Murray wrote, "The Hawkeyes didn't win the Rose Bowl, but they gave the ones who did fits...if you like guys who keep fighting when they are surrounded, you got to go for the Hawkeyes."

Murray, whose latter years were filled with tragedy (the death of a wife and a son, and eventual blindness), could write movingly of the sadder side of sports. On the sudden death of college basketball star Hank Gathers: "Death should stay away from young men's games. Death belongs in musty hospital rooms, sickbeds. It should not impinge its terrible presence on the celebrations of youth; reap its frightful harvest in fields where cheers ring and bands play and banners wave."

Murray won every award his profession and his peers can offer: a Pulitzer Prize, Baseball Hall of Fame, and national "Sportswriter of the Year" fourteen times.

I have great respect for the print media and the job they have to do—partly because, although I have made my living as a "talker," I started off as a writer. (I was Editor-in-Chief of *The*

Daily Iowan while at Iowa, and was writing scripts for CBS in Chicago when I was 21, before coming to WHO).

There has been a vast change in the print media and the way they cover stories, especially the games themselves. Television—and I like to think radio, too—have turned it all around. Today, the fans have seen and heard everything as it happens, on and off the field, 12 hours before the first newspaper hits the streets. Sportswriters have had to change their whole approach; go for "inside" stories, become more inventive and adversarial. This has not always made them the coaches' best friend.

I remember the "thundering" leads of Bert McGrane in describing Iowa football in the Sunday *Register* Big Peach, and the on-the-scene locker room reports of Tony Cordaro. In those days we all travelled together on the Rock Island Rocket—going to games in faraway places like Columbus, Ohio, and Ann Arbor, Michigan, and impossible-to-get-to places like Bloomington and West Lafayette, Indiana, and Champaign, Illinois. Bert and Tony (and the myriad of other 'big-time' sports writers like John Carmichael and Arch Ward of Chicago) were my heroes.

With Bob Earle and Ed Podolak

I'll never forget one night in Columbus before the infamous 1950 Iowa-Ohio State game, the local NBC station there invited Bert and me to go on television and talk about next day's game. They asked us to pick a final score. I forget what Bert picked, but I chose Iowa to win 21-14. I was halfway right. Iowa did get 21 points. Ohio State got 83, in what still stands as the largest blowout in the history of the series. For me, as a young guy just starting out, it was a 'baptism by fire' in the world of big-time college football.

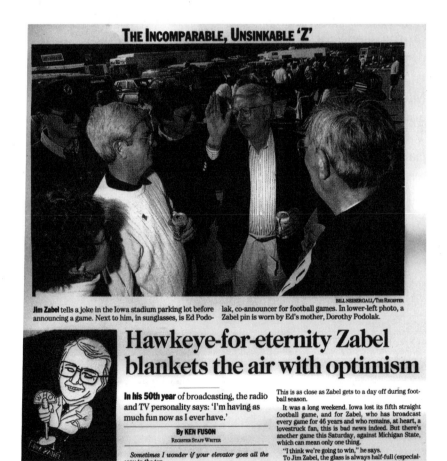

THE INCOMPARABLE, UNSINKABLE 'Z'

BILL NEIBERGALL/THE REGISTER

Jim Zabel tells a joke in the Iowa stadium parking lot before announcing a game. Next to him, in sunglasses, is Ed Podo-lak, co-announcer for football games. In lower-left photo, a Zabel pin is worn by Ed's mother, Dorothy Podolak.

Hawkeye-for-eternity Zabel blankets the air with optimism

In his 50th year of broadcasting, the radio and TV personality says: 'I'm having as much fun now as I ever have.'

By KEN FUSON
REGISTER STAFF WRITER

Sometimes I wonder if your elevator goes all the

This is as close as Zabel gets to a day off during football season.

It was a long weekend. Iowa lost its fifth straight football game, and for Zabel, who has broadcast every game for 46 years and who remains, at heart, a lovestruck fan, this is bad news indeed. But there's another game this Saturday, against Michigan State, which can mean only one thing.

"I think we're going to win," he says.

To Jim Zabel, the glass is always half-full (especial-

Photo printed with permission by the Des Moines Register

Chapter 4

BASKETBALL DAYS

Early Times—Ben Trickey grabs a rebound

Heartstoppers & Heartbreakers

THE FABULOUS FIVE:
FINAL FOUR AND MORE

Iowa's legendary "Fabulous Five" basketball team played in back-to-back Final Fours in 1955 and 1956. They played San Francisco and Bill Russell for the NCAA Championship in 1956. The "Fabulous Five" was a collection of five sophomores (Bill Logan, Carl Cain, Bill Seaberg, Sharm Scheuerman, Bill Schoof) who amazed everyone with their slick ball-handling ability, fast break offense and deadly shooting.

They came into being on February 22, 1954, at Bloomington, Indiana.

The previous Saturday Iowa had lost to Johnny Kerr and Illinois 74-51 in Iowa City. Coach Bucky O'Connor was so irate on the postgame show I did with him that he announced he was going to completely revamp his lineup for the next game, starting four sophomores—Logan, Cain, Seaberg and Scheuerman and a junior, McKinley "Deacon" Davis (who alternated with Schoof at forward.) The "next game," it so happened, was against the defending national-champion Indiana Hoosiers, at

One of Iowa's greatest teams: the Fabulous Five with Coach Bucky O'Connor

Bloomington on Monday. The Hoosiers returned all five starters from their championship year, headed by All-Americans Don Schlundt and Bobby Leonard, and Hall-Of-Fame Coach Branch McCracken.

So we flew to Bloomington on Sunday and got ready for the game Monday night. I feared the worst. After all, here were our "babes in the woods" against their grizzled veterans, playing in front of one of the toughest crowds in collegiate basketball.

The game was one of the most incredible I have ever witnessed by an Iowa team. Indiana could not handle Iowa's fast-break offense which they had never seen before. I remember Bobby Leonard, who later became an all-pro guard, throwing up his hands in despair. McCracken was so frustrated he pulled his starters at the end after Iowa had built a 20-point lead. The Hawkeyes won the game 82-64, and a legend was born.

The Fabulous Five finished second in the Big 10 that year, then they won the title the next two and made it to the Final Four each time. These were the days when only the first place team in the league went to the NCAA Tournament.

The Hawkeyes won 17 of their first 21 games in 1955, then advanced to the NCAA Mideast Regional, where they beat Penn State and Marquette in the opening round. After that, it was off to Kansas City and the Final Four. Iowa was paired against La Salle and its superstar, Tom Gola. In the other game, it was Colorado against San Francisco and the most talked about player in the country, Bill Russell, who was just a junior.

We got our first up-close look at Russell at the NCAA pre-game press conference. He stood about 6-10, but what impressed you the most was his arm-span and size of his hands. ("They were like backboards," Bill Logan later said. "He could reach out and swat shots you'd swear nobody could touch." As a matter of fact the NCAA put in the offensive and defensive goal-tending rules on the basis of Russell's performance in Kansas City).

An *Associated Press* photographer showed me a photo he had taken the week before at the NCAA Regional in Corvallis, Oregon. He had Russell pose with Swede Halbrooke of Oregon State, the tallest player in collegiate basketball at 7- feet 2- inches. He said, "I asked Halbrooke to hold the ball by his fingertips as high as he could. Then I asked Russell to reach up and try and touch the ball, like he was going for the tip. Russell brought his arm up and up and up, and finally put his hand on <u>top</u> of the ball. I wouldn't have believed it if I hadn't seen it."

The Hawkeyes played a good game against La Salle, but lost to Tom Gola's team by 3 points. San Francisco completely dominated Colorado in the first game. They went on to whip La Salle for the 1955 NCAA Championship.

The 1956 season began with great anticipation. We were all shocked when the Hawkeyes dropped three straight games on the West Coast to Washington, Stanford and California, and

Logan goes up, up almost as high as Bill Russell

then lost their Big 10 opener to Michigan State by one point, 66-65. "We were not in sync," Logan said. "Bucky called a team meeting at his home. We got some personal differences off our chest, and got back to concentrating on basketball. Bucky was a great psychologist. We all felt better after the meeting."

The Hawkeyes then raced through the rest of the season with 14 straight victories. The biggest game was against arch-rival Illinois on March 3, 1956. The tension was heightened by a personal vendetta that Illinois Coach Harry

Combes had waged against the Hawkeyes. He charged that Iowa was raiding Illinois for players, and he vowed to show no mercy when the teams met. (The truth is that Logan was the only Hawkeye recruited by Combes, and he is from Keokuk, Iowa.) There were 5,000 people lined up waiting to get in when I came through the door at the Fieldhouse. The game was on national TV. It

Bill Logan hands off to Carl Cain

was close for one half, then Iowa blew it open in the second half, winning 96-72. Combes groused after the game, "It took Illinois players to beat us."

The Hawkeyes next headed for the NCAA Regional, which was held in Iowa City. (The NCAA was looking for attendance in those days, so it allowed host schools to play in their own Regional.) Iowa beat Morehead State in the opener, then they met Adolph Rupp's mighty Kentucky Wildcats in the next game. Iowa won 89-77. Next stop: The Final Four at Evanston.

The Hawkeyes' first opponent was Temple, boasting the famed guard tandem of Lear and Rodgers. Iowa won 83-76.

Now came the big moment—a showdown meeting with San Francisco for the NCAA title. I remember the night vividly. Alex Drier had me on his NBC network news show, and I interviewed the mayor of San Francisco.

The Hawks actually fared very well in the early going against their fearsome opponent. Iowa led 14-4 after the first seven minutes. "Then San Francisco called a time-out," Logan later joked, "and Russell decided to take off his warm ups."

Gradually, San Francisco closed the gap, and finally took the lead behind the awesome play of Russell. ("He was everywhere," Logan said, "It's tough to shoot when you have to keep one eye on that big guy.") Russell grabbed 27 rebounds, an all-time NCAA record. Iowa stayed competitive most of the way, but in the end it was San Francisco 83-71.

This was Russell's second straight NCAA title. He went on to win eleven NBA championships. Even in defeat, the Fabulous Five etched their names among the greats in Iowa sports history. Their play electrified fans for three years.

After the game, I interviewed Bill Russell's father. While he was happy about his son being named MVP, he was proudest of the contract he was about to sign with the Boston Celtics. "It's the richest contract of all time," the senior Russell said. "Thirty-five thousand dollars a year!"

I often think of that interview these days when I read about the latest payday amounts for LeBron, Shaq and Kobe.

P.S.—Coach Bucky O'Connor was killed in an auto accident in 1958 while on his way to a speaking engagement in Waterloo. The funeral for the popular young coach was one of the saddest moments I can remember in Hawkeye athletics.

Interviewing Billy Packer

LUTE, LUTE, LUTE, AND BOBBI
A CELEBRATION TO REMEMBER

Bobbi Olson was noted for her sparkling personality and delicious apple pancakes. Both were powerful recruiting tools for husband Lute. Bobbi had the knack of making you feel you were the only person in the room. She could be flirtatious and vivacious. At one particularly giddy moment I said to her, "Bobbi, suppose everyone else in the world would die, and you and I were the only two left on earth. What would you do?" She said, with a sly smile, "I'd kill myself." Bobbi was something else. Mainly, she was the power behind the throne her husband occupied.

Lute Olson arrived on the Iowa scene in 1975, following four topsy-turvy years with Dick Schultz. Iowa's 1973 season was one of the weirdest I have ever covered. The Hawkeyes beat both Kentucky and Kansas on the road (who ever does that?). And on top of that, they defeated conference champion Minnesota twice, but they finished last in the Big 10.

Lute Olson and wife, Bobbi

How could that be? Schultz had a big, slow team (Kevin Kunnert, Jim Collins, Neil Fegebank) that could beat other big, slow teams, but had trouble with the small, quick ones.

I remember the Kentucky game. They were in a brand-new arena and they had a special courtside seat—more like a throne—for their legendary ex-coach, Adolph Rupp. I interviewed him just before the game. Most people don't realize that he got his start at Marshalltown High School, coaching girls basketball. Rupp told me (exact words), "I like coming to the games, but I wish people would stop asking me for autographs."

Schultz was fired after the 1974 season, which produced an 8-16 record. His career actually blossomed after that. He became athletic director at Cornell (New York), then at Virginia, and after that he was named to the highest post in collegiate athletics—Executive Director of the NCAA.

Iowa began its search for a new coach. There was a brief flurry of interest in bringing Ralph Miller back from Oregon State, fanned by a die-hard group of Miller backers, but Athletic Director Bump Elliott wanted to start out fresh with someone new. (Actually, I feel that Bump did not want to open old wounds by bringing back any vestige of the Evashevski era and run the risk of dividing the fan base again).

An attorney in Los Angeles, who was an Iowa grad, became a major player in the coaching sweepstakes. His name was Al Schallau and his candidate was Lute Olson, most recently of Long Beach State, where he followed the infraction-plagued regime of Jerry Tarkanian. Lute wanted out. (In fact, Bobbi later told me he was about ready to go into real estate.)

Schallau, who is a sports activist and a Hawkeye through and through (although he also holds a degree from USC) sang the praises of Lute Olson, and Bump listened.

After a visit to the Iowa campus, Lute became Coach Olson and started a nine-year run in Iowa City. Lute and Bobbi were a glamorous couple and they became the toast of Hawkeyeland. Fan interest was at an all-time high. The Iowa Television Network came on the scene and created a frenzied following for Hawkeye basketball that lasted for decades.

Lute struggled the first few years, but he was a tireless recruiter. (I can remember one time we flew into East Lansing, Michigan in a blinding snowstorm. Lute climbed right back on the chartered plane to fly back to Chicago and scout Isiah Thomas).

Top: Lute and Hawkeye fans

Center: Bobbi Olson (right) and best friend Bobbie Stehbens

Bottom: Bobbi Olson and friends in Iowa City

Finally, he got the team he wanted. I thought it was one of Iowa's best—Ronnie Lester, Bobby Hansen, Vince Brookins, Kenny Arnold, Kevin Boyle, Mark Gannon and the "Twin Towers" of Waite and Krafcisin.

The Hawkeyes roared into the 1980 NCAA Tournament and knocked off Virginia Commonwealth and North Carolina State in the first round. Then it was on to the Sweet 16 and dramatic wins over perennial powers Syracuse and Georgetown, the latter victory (81-80) coming on a spectacular shot by Steve Waite.

The Hawkeyes were welcomed back to the loudest celebration ever heard in old Iowa Fieldhouse (at least in my time)—15,000 fans were jammed to the rafters. Their thunderous ovation actually honored two Hawkeye teams. Fans were also welcoming Dan Gable's wrestlers, who had just won the National Championship. I even got on the mike myself to lead a few cheers, encouraged by "The Jim Zabel Fan Club" which the wild-and-crazy Dan Pomeroy helped to establish. It was truly a celebration to remember!

The great season of 1980 had a sad post-script. The Hawkeyes lost to Louisville in the Final Four at Indianapolis, 80–72. I still maintain that Iowa would have won the title if Ronnie Lester had not injured his knee in a Christmas tournament at Dayton. (Red Auerbach told me in a halftime interview at Dayton that Ronnie Lester was the best guard he had seen that year and would play 15 years in the NBA. That was before we knew the seriousness of Ronnie's injury).

The game that many fans probably remember most vividly is Iowa at Purdue in 1982—better known as "The Jim Bain Game". Lute contended it was a "phantom foul" on Iowa called by Bain that gave the Boilermakers a 66-65 victory. The Iowa coach was so furious he could hardly do the postgame radio show I did with him. His anger carried over to his TV show the next day, which we taped at our WHO-TV studios in Des Moines.

With Lute "incognito"

Our switchboard was jammed to overflowing with irate calls. People wanted to know the phone number for the Big 10 office in Chicago. So I gave it out. Several hours later Big 10 Commissioner Wayne Duke called. He was as angry as Lute. "Our phone lines are swamped," he fumed, "because you gave out the damn number!" I explained, "I gave it out because everyone wanted to know it, and we couldn't handle the calls."

Bad feelings simmered for a long time, from all sides. Lute was mad. Wayne Duke was mad. I was mad. And Jim Bain was pretty much running for cover.

Duke laughs about it now, but he still remembers it, almost 30 years later. "I never got so many damn calls and letters in my life," he told me in 2009. "Thousands of them!" I have known Wayne for 40 years, we are still good friends. I had him on my radio show in December 2009.

Lute received a number of coaching offers during his career. He turned down the Southern Cal job after keeping Iowa guessing for weeks. His decision came as we were getting ready to play Indiana at Bloomington. I had just finished recording his pregame radio show in his motel room. The past week Lute had been involved in some back-and-forth media talk about USC. Brent Musburger, who was doing a TV sports show in

After a great victory

Los Angeles, reported that Lute had taken the Southern Cal job. Lute publicly called Musburger "a liar." I pointed out to Lute that the story, as big as we might think it was, appeared on page eight of the *Los Angeles Times.* (Basketball was still running a distant second to football in the L.A. market. It was a fact that attendance averaged about 1,200 for Trojan games.) Two days later, Lute announced he was staying at Iowa.

On another occasion, Arizona State made a pitch for Lute. I had put him in touch with ASU athletic director Dick Tamburo, whom I had known when he was assistant football coach at Iowa. He had called me, asking my help in contacting Lute. They met, but could not agree on terms. Lute told me a number of years later at an Arizona—ASU game, "Just think, if they had loosened their purse strings a little, I might have been sitting on the other bench."

Departure time for Lute came on a snowy night in Kansas City in 1983. The Hawkeyes had just lost their NCAA Midwest Regional game by one point to Villanova and Rollie Massimino (one of the few truly unbearable coaches I have ever known).

I was doing Lute's postgame show, when something strange happened. Lute was always a lengthy interview but this night he went even longer. We talked at least 25 minutes. Something flashed into my mind—was this Lute's swan song? He couldn't seem to let go. (I remember what Bobbi had told me several weeks before. I jokingly asked her if she had decided where she wanted Lute to coach if he left Iowa. She replied, "I can't tell you. But I know one thing. There will be palm trees outside the window." There it was! The clue. In retrospect, I should have figured it out.)

Lute finished his coach's show and headed for Tucson to take the Arizona job. His 25 years there have produced a national championship, a record number of victories and Pac 10 titles, an all-time mark for NCAA appearances and election to the Hall of Fame. They also produced the saddest moment in Lute Olson's life.

The exact time was one minute after midnight, on January 1, 2001. That was the precise moment of Bobbi Olson's death. Her funeral lasted two hours. Everyone was there.

I could not help but think this not only marked the end of Lute and Bobbi as one of America's most attractive and popular sports couples, but also of the Lute Olson dynasty. Sure, the myth, the records and the legend would live on, but not the magic of the man himself.

Lute fired his assistant of 34 years, Jim Rosborough. He took a leave of absence, then retired from his coaching job, he had a stroke, a bad second marriage and a bitter divorce.

I could not help but think of the admonition that "life is a play with a lousy third act." Then I thought that perhaps in his case the fates would be kinder. After all, here was a man who achieved more in his lifetime, and reached greater heights, than most can hope for. He was honored by his players and thousands of his fans when he returned to Kinnick Stadium in the fall of 2009. More honors followed around the Pac-10. And he is revered when he attends Arizona home games.

His life is still that of a champion, and he no longer has to worry about losing.

PORTRAIT OF A CONTENTED MAN

Sports columnist Paola Boivin, covered Lute Olson's induction into the Arizona Sports Hall of Fame on April 8, 2010, and wrote this in the *Arizona Republic*, "He looked great. Fit, dapper and turning on the charm that worked so well in the homes of recruits. His voice was a little softer, his words a little more deliberate, but everything else seemed the same as he addressed a large crowd in a light-hearted 10-minute speech.

Things must be going well. He's heading to Hawaii to marry his girlfriend, Tucson resident Kelly Pugnea, next weekend at The Bay Course in Kapalua.

"I feel great, I really do", Olson, 75, said. "I had health issues and it was hard, but I'm doing fine now."

Lute and bride

MILLER TIME!
HAWKEYE HOOPS BONANZA

Ralph Miller's 1970 Iowa Basketball Team averaged 102 points a game in Big 10 play. Think about that! <u>Averaged 102 points!</u> Fred Brown, John Johnson, Glenn Vidnovic, Chad Calabria and company were an offensive machine—the most exciting scoring unit I have ever covered.

Ralph himself was as colorful as the team he coached. A great college athlete, he starred in three sports at Kansas—football, basketball and track. He set records in all three.

After that, he coached Wichita East to the Kansas State High School Championship, then moved on to Wichita State where he won the Missouri Valley Conference title. That caught the attention of Hawkeye Athletic Director Forest Evashevski, who hired Miller at Iowa.

Ralph's personality could frighten the faint-of-heart. He was gruff and tough, often growling his answers when you asked him a question. He was also a brilliant basketball tactician, and he didn't mind letting you know.

Ralph Miller—one of the best

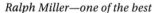

"Go Get UCLA!"

I remember the time we were playing UCLA at Chicago Stadium. The Bruins were defending National Champions under coach John Wooden and they went on to win the title again that season, with standout players like Gail Goodrich and Keith Erickson.

It was 10 degrees below zero when we boarded the team bus for Chicago Stadium. I sat next to Ralph on the bus. I got up my nerve and asked him what he really thought about the game. Ralph gave me a look of absolute disdain and said, almost in a snarl, "We're going to win...if they follow my game plan. Wooden's never beaten me!"

He was right. His record against Wooden was 2-0. He was right about the game , too! On that chilly night in Chicago, with guys like George Peeples, Chris Pervall, Jerry Jones and Jimmy Rodgers leading the way, Iowa played the powerful Bruins to a standstill. I was broadcasting courtside near the UCLA bench, and I could see that superstars Goodrich and Erickson were completely frustrated.

Iowa won the game 78-72. I couldn't believe it! I said that to Ralph going back on the team bus. It was now 15 degrees below zero. There was that look of utter disdain again. Ralph growled, "Of course we won! They followed my game plan!"

Think of it—3-0 against the winningest coach in history!

One of the more interesting highlights of the evening came at halftime of the Iowa-UCLA game. My interview guest was Oral Roberts, the man himself, live and in person. His namesake school was playing Loyola of Chicago in the second game of the basketball double-header.

We talked about the religious aspects of his school, then I asked, "Does divine guidance help you win basketball games?" He said, "No, good shooters do."

At the end of the interview, I asked, "Suppose I had a headache, what would you do to cure it?" Without saying a word, he placed his hand on my forehead and said, "See, you feel better."

My headache was gone—but then, I didn't have one in the first place. He anticipated my answer, saying "Now you won't get a headache even if you lose the game. If you win, I'll put my hand on Coach Wooden's head."

Two one-point games defined the best and the worst of the 1970 season, which turned out to be Ralph Miller's last at Iowa.

On Feb. 28, 1970, Iowa and Purdue played one of the classic Big 10 games of all time, in Mackey Arena at West Lafayette. Boilermaker star Rick Mount poured in 63 points (before the day of the 3-point shot) but Iowa won the game at the buzzer 108–107.

The Hawkeyes needed to win only two more games, against Ohio State and Northwestern, to become only the second team in Big 10 history to go through the cnference season undefeated. The Hawkeyes won both games. Then it was on to the NCAA Tournament in Columbus, Ohio and that infamous game with Jacksonville which had a 7-foot frontline.

Remember Artis Gilmore and Pembroke Burrows the Third? I will never forget them. Iowa got down by 12 points late in the second half, then came storming back as if they suddenly realized "Hey, we can beat these guys."

That brought the game down to the last dramatic shot. Freddie Brown took one of his patented downtown shots, but missed. Instead of bouncing back to the perimeter, the ball hung there, and Pembroke Burrows grabbed it with those long arms of his. Final score: Jacksonville 104, Iowa 103.

I was devastated. So was my color man, former Iowa Coach Sharm Scheuerman.

Ralph never forgot that game; neither did the players. Years later, when they were pros, I talked with John and Fred, and they both thought they should have beaten Jacksonville. Sidney Wicks of UCLA told me he thought the Hawkeyes could have won the National Championship that year. In a rare show of remorse, Ralph said he felt he had "overscouted" Jacksonville. "I kept telling our guys how great Jacksonville was because of their huge front line, and I think we started worrying too much instead of staying loose."

Retroactive feelings aside, Iowa came out with guns blazing in the consolation game against Notre Dame, scoring 75 points in the first half, and winning 121-106.

Shortly before the NCAA Tournament, Ralph confided to me that he was leaving Iowa. I was stunned. We were in his hotel room after taping his pregame show. "How can you do that," I blurted out. "You've just had one of the best seasons in Iowa history!" I have to admit I had grown very fond of Ralph and had tremendous respect for him as a coach. I knew that underneath all of that bluster, there was a generous man with a heart as big as Iowa Fieldhouse.

Ralph said he had already accepted the job at Oregon State. He explained that with Evashevski about to go, which was common knowledge, he didn't feel good about his own future since he was hired by Evy. "Jean (his wife) and I love Iowa City, but I think this is the best way to do it. Nobody gets hurt." So that was that. Ralph was tremendously popular with the fans, but I really think the continuing turmoil in the athletic department was getting to him.

What a resume this man compiled in his lifetime! The championship of three major conferences—Big 10, Pac-10 and Missouri Valley—plus the Kansas state high school title while at Wichita East.

He was one of the best! I think Johnny Wooden would agree with that.

HAWKEYE SNAPSHOTS

Chuck Long
Photo printed with permission by the Des Moines Register

I was in Chicago to broadcast an Iowa-Northwestern basketball game, and I got a call from Chuck Long's father. He wanted me to come to suburban Wheaton to emcee "Chuck Long Day" at Wheaton High School.

They sent a limo to pick me up. When I arrived, there were 3,000 people jammed into the high school gym. They were literally hanging from the rafters. I was told the last time they had a day like that was to honor Red Grange, the "Galloping Ghost," the "Wheaton Ice Man" of Illinois football fame.

Who can ever forget that Michigan State game in 1985 when Chuck faked the ball to Ronnie Harmon, then bootlegged it into the end zone for the winning touchdown. Norm Parker never forgot it. He was the defensive coordinator at Michigan State at the time.

Twenty years later, when Iowa scored on that spectacular 56-yard pass from Drew Tate to Warren Holloway to beat LSU in the 2005 Capital One Bowl, the happiest guy in Iowa City was Norm Parker. "Thank God", Norm says, "I don't have to watch that damn Chuck Long bootleg on ESPN Classic anymore!"

When George Raveling left Iowa for Southern Cal, after the 1986 season, incoming coach Tom Davis was on the stage with him at the Hawkeye basketball banquet. I was serving as emcee of the affair at Iowa Memorial Union. I opened with some strong words for George, who was a guy I really liked. He was a tireless recruiter, a great competitor and fun person to be around. Intellectually and professionally, he was a man for all seasons. Among other things, he subscribed to 125 newspapers because he wrote a weekly column using quotes from coast to coast. I led off the program by saying I did not think George would leave because I couldn't imagine anyone making 125 changes of address.

Tom Davis followed George to the podium and gave a preview of things to come. And what a beginning it was!

The Hawkeyes won their first 18 games, including the Great Alaska Shootout, and then won the first three games in the NCAA Tournament, losing only to eventual NCAA Champion UNLV. I loved that team of Tom Davis', with Horton, Marble, B.J., Lohaus and the guy who I thought was the unsung hero of the team, Kevin Gamble. I felt that with a few breaks, this group could have won it all.

Incidentally, Dick Vitale was the featured speaker at the banquet, one of the few times he ever got outdone in the spoken word department. It was a great night.

Tom Davis spent 14 years at Iowa

PEARL'S WISDOM
SURVIVING THE STORM

Bruce Pearl tapped me on the shoulder as I was broadcasting the Boy's State Basketball Tournament at Veterans Auditorium. I turned around and he said, "Meet me at the Marriott after the game. I've got to talk to you. I'll be in the bar."

I knew what he wanted to talk about. The Iowa assistant coach had been in the headlines the past few weeks because of the Deon Thomas affair. He had taped phone conversations with Thomas in which the Chicago high school star had described inducements that Illinois had allegedly offered in recruiting him. Pearl turned the tapes over to the NCAA, and they handed down various sanctions against the Illini. Instead of hailing him as a hero, a substantial section of the media portrayed him as the villain. Dick Vitale said publicly that Pearl "would never get another job." Illinois fans were furious.

Bruce and I were close. He was my roommate when I went with the basketball team to Korea and China. We traveled together, ate together and shopped together on Itaewon Street in Seoul, where the merchants follow you down the street trying to sell you hand-tailored garments of all types. Bruce was a fun guy. You couldn't help but like him.

But this particular night he was serious. "I had to do it," he told me when we met. "They were wrong. I had to report them."

I explained to Bruce that no one could deny he was right, and many people would privately admire him, but unfortunately, that's not the way the game was played. "There's a lot of the 'Good ol' boy' attitudes in conferences like the Big 10", I said, "You don't tell on me, and I won't tell on you. That's the kind of system you're bucking."

"It's wrong!" Bruce declared. "I'm not trying to be holier-than-thou, I just want to have an even chance when I'm recruiting a kid."

I told Bruce I was proud of him, and so were a lot of other people, but that he would pay a price. And, for a while he did. But if Bruce is anything, he is determined.

The immediate repercussions were anything but enjoyable. We took a bus the next time we played Illinois in Champaign, spending the night in nearby Peoria. When we finally arrived at Assembly Hall, it was like an armed camp. There were police all over the place. Even the highway patrol was on duty.

The ROTC Unit came out to present the colors before the game, and the crowd grew quiet. The sergeant gave his command— "Present Arms." Then someone in the crowd shouted, "Shoot Iowa!"

The Illinois team apparently took their cue from that, because they rolled over the Hawkeyes—118-85. (The Hawkeyes got revenge in football in 1990, walloping the Illini 54-28.)

Pearl himself defied the naysayers. After a series of small-college jobs, where he continued to win, Bruce turned Wisconsin-Milwaukee into a basketball power. Next, it was off to Tennessee, where he turned a traditional football giant into a basketball headliner as well.

Think of it: After losing his top scorer, Tyler Smith, for disciplinary reasons, he managed to beat two No. 1 ranked teams (Kentucky and Kansas) within days of each other in 2010 and made it to the Elite 8 of the NCAA before losing by one point to Michigan State. Not bad for the kid who started out as a mascot for Tom Davis' Boston College team. There seems to be no limit to what this coaching dynamo can do.

Chapter 5

DES MOINES DAYS

How You Gonna Keep 'Em Down on the Farm After They've Seen Des Moines

FUN CITY USA
D.M. AT MID-CENTURY

Des Moines in the 1940s had it all—all-night bars, all-star entertainment and the all-encompassing presence of 5,000 WACs. It also had an all-star cast of characters running the show. Topping the list was Alphonse "Babe" Bisignano, whose 6th Ave. establishment was known by servicemen coast to coast. Babe's was actually a three-tiered affair—a restaurant and bar downstairs, a 400-person nightclub upstairs (where George Gobel and Roger Williams once entertained), and an adjoining venue where drinking, dancing and occasionally gambling prevailed, known as the Jungle Club. Babe was a colorful ex-boxer/wrestler with the hands of a stonecutter and a personality right out of "Guys and Dolls". (In fact, he once played Big Julie in the Des Moines Playhouse production of the Broadway classic.)

Other prominent members of the Des Moines night life scene and their places of business were Johnny Compiano (Johnny and Kay's), his brother Rocky (White Shutter Inn), Tony Sestini (Venetian Room), Vic Talerico (Vic's Tally-Ho), Johnny Stamatelos (Vets Club, West Des Moines), Frankie Rand (Tally Rand Club), Dave Fidler (Bar & Lounge at 6th & Grand), Johnny and Tony Critelli (Critelli's at the corner of Hickman & Harding Road, and Critelli's Sho-Bar downtown), and Rocky Gabriel (Office Lounge). All of these places had entertainment, drinks and food. There also was the Chesterfield Club, where I saw singer Frances Langford. John Cimino ran Wimpy's and featured prime steaks served by male waiters in tuxedos. Warren's Steakhouse on Fleur Drive likewise served memorable cuts of beef.

But the classiest spot was the Victorian Room at Johnny and Kay's. Modeled after Ernie's in San Francisco, it had red frieze wallpaper and Barbary Coast fixtures. Kay Compiano would entertain us with her songs, and husband Johnny would provide us with delicious food.

If you wanted to meet sports celebrities, servicemen and WACs (on Saturday nights, lots of them) you went to Babe's. One of my favorite spots was the Tally Rand Club, at 3rd & Grand, where Speck Redd's Combo was playing. (I first saw him at the Rendezvous Club in Moline) If you wanted a Las Vegas-type show place, the Mainliner, run by Pete Rand, was the spot. Frank Sinatra once performed there after he left Tommy Dorsey. (Pete showed me the cancelled check.) Mommies was a swinging place down by the Kirkwood Hotel, and right next to the Fort Des Moines Hotel there was a nightclub that has special meaning for me. It was called the Green Parrot and the young guy you would have found playing the piano there late at night is one of my best friends today—Al McCoy, the Hall-of-Fame voice of the Phoenix Suns basketball team. Al and I worked together at WHO while he was going to Drake. He played piano with Don Hoy's band on weekends, and during the week at the Parrot. He is a talented jazz pianist.

Speaking of music, the big band era reached its absolute peak in Des Moines. Tom Archer owned 12 ballrooms across the Midwest, two of them—Val Air and the Tromar—in Des Moines. (Val Air is still around, in West Des Moines, but the Tromar, at 6th and Keo, is gone.) All of the big bands played Des Moines—Miller, Dorsey, Goodman, Shaw, and all the rest—it was a fabulous time. One date I will never forget is May 31, 1942. A bunch of us came up from Iowa City to see Glenn Miller at Val Air Ballroom. He drew a record crowd of 4,000. Believe it or not, admission was one dollar. (It was the tail end of the Depression.) I got a call from Tom Archer one day, inviting me to lunch with Tommy Dorsey. It was fascinating hearing first-hand how Dorsey and Sinatra produced No. 1 hits like "I'll Never Smile Again".

Dave Fidler's lounge was popular with the *Register* crowd and other media types. (In fact, *Register* managing editor Frank Eyerly made me a job offer there once. I told him I would take the job if I could broadcast the games first, then write. No dice.) Dave was an ex-boxer with a great sense of humor. He also ran the 100 Club, next to the Val Air Ballroom, a Las Vegas style casino and night club. Dave became a good friend (I was a pall bearer at his funeral).

One night I went to Sasto Battani's on 6th Ave. He had fan dancer Sally Rand performing there. She had created a sensation at the World's Fair in Chicago years before. She had to be in her 70s but could still whip those fans around.

Remember Al De Carlo? He had a big restaurant and night club north of town on 6th Ave. called the Casa Loma Club where Drake used to hold its basketball banquets. I was MC one time when Babe was there. He was a big Drake fan and a good friend of De Carlo's. They did a routine where they would get into a loud argument then stage a phony fight, with one slapping his hands together while the other would pretend to punch him. It was so realistic that the Drake captain said, "I'm getting the hell out of here!" I had to go out to the parking lot to assure him it was just a gag.

It was always a big night when Evashevski came to town. One Sunday night Al Couppee came over to WHO-TV after Evy and I had finished his TV show. Evy said he was hungry, but it was late on Sunday night and every place was closed. I called the White Shutter Inn on Fleur and caught Rocky just as he was leaving. He said, "Sorry, but we're closed." I explained that Evy was with me and he was hungry. Rocky said, "Come on out. I'll heat up the grill." We had some of the best steaks I have ever tasted. Rocky even fried some of his peppers for us. Such was the power of Evashevski in those days.

A couple of places I loved to go to were Geno's on 6th Ave. (Geno used to be head chef at Johnny and Kay's) and Christopher's in Beaverdale (I did all of their commercials for 35 years, and Joe Giudicessi, the owner, was always amazed at the power and scope of WHO Radio, especially when people from all over the state would come in). I ate there so often that his son, Ron, kept a taxi hat over the bar and would run me home if I was enjoying myself too much. Ron liked to listen to Sinatra on my

Zenith wedge LP player. In fact, when we sold our Beaverdale home in 2009, my wife and I donated the wedge and the Sinatra LPs to Ron, who is the proprietor of Mezzodi's on Fleur.

Noah's Ark on Ingersoll is still going strong, and I used to love talking with owner Noah Lacona when I was calling a lot of auto races because he was a sports car race driver. He also has the best spaghetti and meatballs in town. Other favorite spots through the years were/are The Latin King, Maxies, Skip's, Scarpino's and the Silhouette. Believe it or not, Dutch Reagan's beloved Moonlight Inn on the west edge of Des Moines was still doing business when I came to town. Cy Griffith, owner and operator, was still on hand, and there was that famous poster-sized picture of Reagan over the bar. (When they tore down Moonlight, Reagan had the entire wall, picture and all, shipped to his home in California.)

The Des Moines I remember in the 1940s had many more hotels than today. In addition to the Fort Des Moines, Savery and Kirkwood, which are still around today, there were the Chamberlain, the Franklin, the Victoria, the Plaza, the Brown and the Commodore. All of them had cocktail lounges, restaurants and, along with Younkers' tea room, were popular gathering places.

Like most cities in America at that time, Des Moines had a black-and-tan entertainment section. It was located on Center Street just off Keo, and was known as "The Stem." (Because of the freeway construction, little remains today). There were a string of night spots noted for their hot jazz and all-out jitterbug dancing. They included the Sepia Club, where the Irene Myles band played, the Billiken Club, where Speck Redd held forth, and the Watkins Hotel Lounge. Some of the great Des Moines jazz artists of that era who performed there were Bobby Parker, Ross Cornelison, Don East, Helen Gale, Francis Bates, Rose Marie Webster, Scott Smith, who is still performing in Des Moines (remember those great "Captain's Cabin" days?). Howard and Seymor Gray did much to promote jazz music as owners of the Sepia Club, and Jim Oatts and his Big Band have

*With Babe Bisignano
(left) and Murray Wier
(middle)*

Babe with Jim and Jill

*Above: Wayne and Wendy Cooley with Jim
and Jill*

*Right: Al McCoy, Voice of the Phoenix Suns
and—a part of the Des Moines scene*

been fixtures on the Des Moines scene for 50 years. Then there are Ben Harrison, Jim Bowermaster, and most of all, my dear friend Ford Roberts, who did so much to bring big band and jazz music into all of our homes. In short, Des Moines has a wonderful musical past.

My roots in Des Moines go deep into history, but one person who remembers the old days along with me is the man I call Pal Joey—Joe Yacavona. I first met Joe when he worked at Babe's, and later on when he had his own place on 5th Ave. in downtown Des Moines. After that he opened a sports bar called Pal Joey's, at 63rd and Grand, which quickly became the in spot for coaches and fans alike. I would meet sports celebrities like Bill Reichardt there. Fans of both Iowa and Iowa State, like Curtis Van Veldhuizen and Don Polite, would drop by. Maybe even Gary Kirke and Bill Krause, but not together. Assistant coaches from everywhere made Pal Joey's their headquarters while recruiting in Des Moines. I was friends with them all, and Pal Joey became my close friend through the years (and his mother made the best fried peppers I have ever tasted).

I am proud of Des Moines today with its shiny new buildings and impressive financial towers. But part of me still yearns for Babe's and Dave Fidler's and Irene Myles playing her marvelous piano at Johnny and Kay's and the Savery Lounge. Des Moines is great today, but I remember a time when Des Moines had it all.

L-R: Murray Wier, Hayden Fry, Babe, Shirley Fry

AFTERNOON TOMFOOLERY
TALK SHOW MANIA

Duane Ellett and friend

The funniest guy I ever worked with—and probably the most talented—was Duane Ellett. He gained his first notoriety on WHO-TV where he entertained generations of children with his famed dog Floppy, but he was equally outstanding on radio, and much more diversified.

Duane and I worked together for years on the "Call Jim Zabel" Show, and I was never quite sure who he was going to be when he came on from the announcer's booth. He created an unforgettable stable of characters. One of my favorites was Maurice Chevrolet, the aging French movie star whom Ellett did with a perfect accent.

Then there was the old-time boxing promoter, K.O. Pectate, who was traveling around the country trying to legalize the low blow.

After I had given a long Christmas recipe which wound up with a concoction called the "Farce," Ellett called as Irish police Captain Patrick Vulgarity, and in a proper Irish brogue accused me of making fun of the boys down on the "Farce," including his assistant, Tiny Minority.

When President Reagan was in China, Ellett came on as the Chinese restaurant owner One Long Tongue, and in an authentic Oriental accent he described the President eating noodles with chopsticks, and after that he did Reagan telling how much he enjoyed the meal ("Well, yes, it was very good what little bit I could get on top of the chopsticks.")

Ellett and I did two news anchors, Wes Pakistan and Les Government, and after a Sears commercial about draperies, we became London barristers Pleats and Seams.

I did a Dr. Scholl's foot commercial once in which I talked about treating a poppaloma—so next Ellett came on with his best Spanish accent as Papa Loma, "The Father of the Bullfight".

Ellett could do a female voice also; in this case Mary McGoon, who was celebrating Halloween with two old friends, Doris Karloff and Della Lagosi.

There was the time when Ellett was working the board and discovered that the Martha Bohlsen Show ran short. So he was asked to fill the five-minute gap before the noon news. Ellett came on as Paul Small with "Teeny Tiny Time." He played "little tiny records," beginning with "There's a Small Hotel."

An irate woman called the show to complain about a bit of political humor I had used. "I'll tell you, Mr. Zabel," she said firmly, "you may think you're funny, but Bob Hope has nothing to worry about!"

I saw Ellett go to the mike. "Hello, Zabel, Bob Hope here", he said, doing a perfect imitation of the comedian. "I just happened to be driving through the countryside and caught your show. I hope you stay in Des Moines because if you come to Hollywood you'll put me out of business."

Ellett's shows from the Iowa State Fair, which he loved doing, were classics. (In 2009 the Fair erected a plaque on the Grand Concourse in his honor.)

On one occasion he demonstrated how to describe fireworks displays and magic tricks on radio.

Ellett: Multi-, multi-bursts of brilliant color...

Floppy: Are you talking about me?

Ellett: I'm describing fireworks.

Floppy: That's beautiful....But how about a magic trick?

Ellett: See this quarter in my hand?

Floppy: I see it.

Ellett: Now you don't. Where is it?

Floppy: In your other hand.

Ellett: You didn't like my magic?

Floppy: Stick with the fireworks. I couldn't see them either. But they sounded prettier.

Of course, his major TV performance at the Fair was always with his faithful dog Floppy, whom the kids adored. One time a youngster got the best of him. He had invited a group of children on TV to tell him their favorite riddles. One kid asked, "What's brown and sits on a piano stool?" The answer, "Beethoven's Last Movement."

Ellett also starred as a singer and announcer (he did it all) on the "Betty Baker Show" which aired early afternoon from the Grand Ballroom of the Savery Hotel. Betty had a way of mixing metaphors and innocently exploiting double meanings, much to the delight of her listeners.

She always had a "question of the day." One day it had to do with hobbies. Her first guest said her hobby was gardening. "I just love to plant a garden and take care of it", she said. "I just get out there and hoe and hoe and hoe, I guess you might call me an old hoer."

Another time her question was "Do you let your husband go out with the boys one night a week?" She talked to one lady guest who explained how much she loved cats. She said she had 10 of them "all over the place." Betty then asked her the question of the day— "Do you let your husband go out with the boys?"

She said, "Yes." Betty asked, "What if he comes home late, is he in the dog house?"

"No," she said, "he's in the cat house."

I loved Betty and so did Ellett.

I did my first "Call Jim Zabel" Show on May 2, 1966. It ran for 2 ½ hours every week day, starting at 1 p.m. Before I went on the air with my first show, I talked with my buddy, Jack Buck, the St. Louis Cardinals broadcaster who also did a daily phone show on KMOX in St. Louis. (I had known Jack since he did Ohio State football in Columbus). Jack told me some of the pitfalls to watch out for. First, he said would be the callers who would want to know my political philosophy. "Be careful how you answer" he said "because what ever position you take, people on the other side will call in and start to blast you, either way you go, you can't win. And another thing: Watch out for the women who want to give you recipes, once that starts, there's no end to it."

Sure enough, my first call was exactly as Jack said. "Zabel, we know you can broadcast sports," the man said "but what are your political views—what side of the fence are you on?" I was ready for him. I said "here is my political philosophy—I am a middle-of-the road extremist." The guy was totally squelched. He mumbled a few words and then hung up.

But that wasn't the end of it. The same guy called again in the next hour of the show (this was before the day of call screeners). He said "Zabel, you know what runs down the middle of the road? A great big yellow line." Bang! He abruptly hung up. My baptism by fire. Welcome to talk radio!

(I got a lot of mileage out of that story. Gov. Terry Branstad invited me to emcee the Jackson Day dinner some years later and I used the story as my lead to assure them I wasn't taking sides).

As time went on I developed a cast of characters, in addition to Ellett, who called on a regular basis.

There was a sweet little lady named Freda Bauers from "down on the Skunk River." Freda had twelve children and a recipe for vegetable soup that she fed them. Then there was George

Preston of Belle Plaine, who collected everything from thresh-ing machines to vintage tractors. ("I can't even get through my own yard," George said.) By far my most expressive caller ("explosive" might be a better word) was Helen Harrington, the famed "Lady from Lamoni." Helen and I argued about prac-tically everything, especially Vietnam. She was vehemently against the war and our presence there. In retrospect, I have to say a lot of people today would have to agree with her.

Despite some pretty hefty debates on the issues of the day, I really tried to keep the show light and breezy. I wanted listen-ers to have fun.

In one respect, I went against Jack Buck's advice—I started tak-ing recipes, but not in the traditional sense. I like to cook and I like unusual off-the-wall recipes. They can be fun to talk about (just look at the number of cooking shows on TV these days).

Strawberry Pop Cake, Vinegar Pie, and Salmon Cooked In A Dishwasher were a few that I put on the air. I met my match with one Thanksgiving-time recipe however. I have always prided myself on being able to look several lines ahead of the copy I am reading. That saved me, because we got so many recipes I would open them on the air and read them cold. I opened this particular recipe and said "look at this—turkey with popcorn dressing—that sounds interesting!"

I started giving the ingredients, "one cup of unpopped pop-corn..." then I looked ahead and virtually collapsed in laughter. I said, "I'm sorry, I can't give the rest of it on the air." The rec-ipe read, "You know it's done when it blows the ass out of the turkey." Wow! Near miss! Even Ellett couldn't contain himself, and we barely made it through the rest of the show.

Actually, the recipe segment paid great dividends. Four years into the show I had accumulated over 6,000 recipes, most called in or sent in by listeners, as well as those I had gotten from restaurants in my travels around the country. With the help of two ladies who published church cookbooks, I put out my first *Jim Zabel's Fabulous Pink Apron Cookbook.* It was a big success. So much so I put out two more editions over the next three years. They sold in all 50 states. I found out one thing: A woman will drive through a blizzard to buy a cookbook. My most requested all-time recipe: Blue Punch. I still get requests for it, particularly in June, for weddings and graduations. So, here it is, exactly as originally published.

Blue Punch

> 1 gal. water
> 11 (6 oz.) cans frozen lemonade
> ½ c. sugar

Mix together, then add food coloring together and add slowly, just 1 scant tablespoon blue coloring, ¼ tablespoon green coloring, just a few drops at a time to shade desired.

Then add:

> 11 (12-oz.) bottles 7-Up
> ½ gal. pineapple sherbet

This recipe serves 50 to 75, depending on size of cups. Could be cut down if necessary.

Of all the celebrity guests I had on the show, one of my favorites was the comedian, George Gobel. He was a great interview and he had a droll sense of humor. We talked for about 30 minutes, then I threw it open to questions from listeners. The first caller, a man, said he was so nervous he couldn't remember what he wanted to say. Gobel told him just to relax and ask his question. The man said, in a quavering voice, "How are all you comedians?" Gobel said "I feel fine. I saw Bob Hope the other day, and he looks good. I ran into Jack Benny and he seems as chipper as ever." Then, after a short pause, "Will Rogers passed away." (Rogers, of course, died in a plane crash in 1936.)

Gobel will be remembered from his appearance on Johnny Carson, when he uttered one of the classic lines in TV history. Johnny Carson was interviewing Gobel when all of a sudden Frank Sinatra, Dean Martin and Bob Hope appeared on the scene. They had been taping a TV special in the next studio. Carson immediately turned his attention to the three super-stars, while Gobel sat silently across the set. Finally, Carson acknowledged George again with a question about his well-being, Gobel replied, "Did you ever feel that the whole world was a tuxedo, and you were a pair of brown shoes?"

Bob Williams, one of our rich-voiced radio and TV announcers, did a popular buy-and-sell show on WHO. He enforced a strict set of rules on the show—no guns, no pets, no cars, no liquor, and so on. Ellett and I decided we would have some fun with him. We told him he was too serious. That he should lighten up a bit and have some fun with his listeners. The next day one of his first calls was from a lady who said she had a blanket for sale. "It's orange and green and purple plaid, Bob." Williams said, "what happened—did your horse die?" The lady replied, "no, my husband did."

Al Bell, our veteran morning announcer on WHO, prided himself on being able to read a copy cold—that is, without having to look it over first. One morning on "Melody Madhouse", he had a commercial for a health insurance company which started out, "If you are injured, who will pay the bills?" The ad agency capitalized the word "WHO" because they wanted it emphasized. So Al Bell read, "If you are injured, W-H-O will pay the bills." Al still managed to keep his job, but I think he went back to corn and soybean commercials.

I did not actually interview Nikita Khrushchev when he visited Roswell Garst's Coon Rapids farm in 1959, but I did cover his comings and goings at the Fort Des Moines Hotel. NBC ran out of reporters to staff the many venues involved in the Soviet leader's history-making visit, so they called on our news department for help. I was stationed at the Fort. I saw Khrushchev perhaps four or five times, as he headed to and from the elevator to the Presidential Suite, usually gesturing and talking to the members of his entourage. He was a short, roly-poly man. The most astounding information I found out about the Russian leader came from a hotel bellhop that I knew. He said, "Khrushchev's main surprise—and the thing that seemed to please him the most—was the fact that he could order a T-bone steak from room service at midnight.

Tommy

Everyone who listens to radio talk shows knows "Tommy." He calls every show regularly. I would estimate that I have taken over 500 calls from him through the years. You can't mistake his voice. In fact, one time he called and said, "You probably won't recognize me. I got a cold." There was no danger of that!

I met Tommy a few years ago in Iowa City, after a game. He loves the Hawkeyes, but he can be a pretty stern critic when things don't go well.

Tommy has his own following. One of his fans was Hayden Fry. Hayden gave him a couple of tickets on the bench once, and Tommy never forgot it. He is unique. Our talk shows would not be quite the same without him.

In Memoriam

Duane Ellett passed away in the summer of 1986. He died of a heart condition while jogging on the high school track in Ankeny. I served as a pallbearer at his funeral.

I think of him, and his immense talent, constantly. Every time something unusual or controversial occurs on television, I wonder how Duane would have handled it, or what clever lines or phrases would have come out, and what Floppy might have said.

Thousands revere his memory. His continuing popularity was demonstrated again by an overflow turnout at the "Duane and Floppy Film Festival" sponsored by the State Historical Society and Wartburg College in December, 2009. All of the showings were sold out, and there were more than 10,000 hits on his website in the last week of December. Wartburg's Jeff Stein served as host of the festival.

I am willing to wager there are thousands of "Duane and Floppy" T-shirts tucked away in closets and cedar chests in Des Moines and central Iowa, and just that many young adults whose childhood memories include tweaking Floppy's nose. God bless them all.

Smooth sailing with Duane and Floppy

CRAZY SUNDAYS

It is not true that God said, "...and on Sundays there shall be a 'Let's Go Bowling Show.'" I am the one who said that. I said it many times during the roughly 20 year span between Forest Evashevski and Hayden Fry. Usually I said it to an I-Club crowd following a long Hawkeye weekend. My exact words were, "Thank God for 'Let's Go Bowling.'" I did the show for 33 years, and it often was the high spot of the weekend in those drab football years between 1960 and 1980.

The show was the brainchild of a group of Des Moines bowling proprietors headed by Pete and Lou Rand, Earl Best, Darrell Thompson and Ed Essy, who were looking for a way to fill their rapidly expanding facilities with new bowlers.

The show was a hit from the beginning. The ratings amazed me. We even beat pro football on CBS when we came on at 12 noon. At its peak, we had 52 Des Moines and Central Iowa bowling establishments on the show. They were sponsors and also served as qualifying locations for bowlers on the show. The standard format was Des Moines against Central Iowa (remember "Let's hear it for the out-of-towners!")

We had a great list of prizes, including a new car for eight strikes in a row. (That's how I first got to know my buddy, Dale Howard of Iowa Falls).

Every now and then we would have all-star shows featuring national pro champions like Don Carter, Dick Weber, Billy Welu, Steve Nagy, Ed Lubanski and Marian Ladewig, the top woman bowler of her day. It was this all-star concept that led to the most disastrous moment in the long history of the show. Normally, "Let's Go Bowling" was seen live on WHO TV for nine months of the year. In the summer, we showed re-runs. One time a major sponsor, Keith Furnace Company, wanted us to do a special all-star show in the middle of summer so they could push some of their air-conditioning products. John Keith

"Let's Go Bowling" on the air for 33 years

Rehmann, head of the company, asked me to "get the biggest pro-bowling name" I could find. I called Brunswick and asked for the top star on their roster who was available. They told me I could have Ned Day, "the grand old man of bowling". In fact, they said, "He practically invented the game." That sounded good to me. I knew of Ned; he was one of the biggest names in the history of the sport. What they didn't tell me about Ned, however, was that he liked to take a nip from the bottle.

We gave the show a lot of advance publicity. Finally the big moment arrived. "Let's Go Bowling" was scheduled to go on live following the major league baseball Game of the Week. My phone rang at home. It was Sue Heefner, who was in charge of qualifying at Plaza Lanes where we were televising the show live. "You better get over here," she said with panic in her voice. I said, "What' s the matter? Didn't our star show up?" She replied, "He showed up all right, but I don't think he knows where he is. He's smashed." I raced over to Plaza Lanes. She was right. Ned had arrived in town the night before and, as far as I could make out, had partied all night. I told him to start drinking black coffee. I was praying for a long TV baseball game, but as luck would have it, it was the shortest game of the year, one hour and 41 minutes. So, I had to make a fast decision. Should we risk putting this guy on in his current condition? I felt we had no choice. We had been promoting the show for three weeks. So I told him not to get up until I asked him to. We hit the opening theme, I explained the format of the show and introduced the local bowlers who were going to compete against Ned Day in a three game series. Then, I announced with great fanfare—"And now, the star of our show, one of the great bowlers of our time—Ned Day—throwing his first ball." Ned got up, unsteadily made his way to the approach, threw his first ball—and fell flat on his face on the lane. He laid there spread-eagled while I searched for words as he scrambled to get up. I said something like, "Those lanes must be really slick today," while I whispered to the floor crew, "For God sake, have the camera pan the scoreboard."

Things went from bad to worse. The next time Ned got up he fell flat on his face again, lying spread-eagled over the foul line. Somehow we made through to the last frame. He had the 7-10 split for his final shot. He got up and took two balls off the rack. He announced, in a slurred voice, "I'm going to criss-cross these balls on the lane and pick up both pins." He then delivered the balls, criss-crossing them on the lane. Both wound up in the gutter. I asked Ned, "How many times have you made that?" Without batting an eye, he said, "Never." We gave Ned the pins from the two fouls and he bowled a 128 in his first game.

The rest of the bowlers were so nervous they didn't do much better. Somehow we made it through the show. As Ned slowly sobered up, his bowling improved. He actually won the final two games. Luckily, he didn't fall again, and even thanked everyone for the "wonderful time" he had in Des Moines. I know one thing—I will never forget my day with Ned Day.

"Let's Go Bowling" had a lot of fans of all ages. I once served as honorary State Mental Health Chairman. As part of my duties, I agreed to tour Woodward State Mental Hospital. While there, I was told the most popular TV show among the inmates was "Let's Go Bowling." I asked "Do they pull for the Des Moines or Central Iowa bowlers?" I was told "Neither. They like the destruction."

"Let's Go Bowling" inspired a number of spin-off projects and events. For a time, I did a TV billiard show, since quite a few of our proprietors had opened billiard parlors. Actually, the game we televised was 15-ball rotation pool. We even had Minnesota Fats on one time. The problem was that your good players would run the table at the top of the show, leaving 15 minutes of interview time. The billiard craze was short-lived, at least as far as TV possibilities were concerned.

I was pleased and honored when the city of Des Moines selected me to lead their 1959 delegation to St. Louis to make a pitch for the National ABC Bowling Tournament, one of the biggest events of its kind since it runs for three months. I emceed the presentation, in competition with four other cities, introducing the mayor and other dignitaries to the ABC delegates. They must have liked what they saw because Des Moines won. The ABC tournament came to Des Moines in 1962, installing 10 bowling lanes in Veterans Auditorium, and playing host to thousands of bowlers from across the country. The Boys and Girls State Basketball Tournaments had to be held elsewhere. (The girls went to Waterloo, the boys to Iowa City.) Drake went back to its own Fieldhouse. It was a great time for the city of Des Moines, and for "Let' s Go Bowling". We had many of the nation's top bowlers on the show.

Another Sunday night staple I did on WHO-TV was "Beat the Bear," which ran off and on for 25 years. It was one of the craziest

Beat the Bear Panel: Randy Duncan, Forest Evashevski, the Bear, and Jim Zabel

shows I was ever connected with. I had done a program called Football Predictions on WHO radio. When TV came along, we moved it there, but with some major changes. First of all the name. How did we ever come up with "Beat the Bear"? Very simple. Hamm's Beer was the sponsor, and they wanted their mascot and logo, the Hamm's Bear, to be a part of the show. Who played the Bear? That was a question I always got. It was usually a member of our staff; By name, Dick Gerdes, Ray Johnson, Al Barcheski and Paul Menzil were the main ones.

Since we covered the Iowa Hawkeyes on WHO radio, our first Bear panel was Forest Evashevski, Randy Duncan, yours truly and the Bear. Then we decided to go to a panel of head coaches from Iowa, Iowa State and Drake, both football and basketball. I remember the night my chair broke, and Coach Earle Bruce of Iowa State could not stop laughing. That blooper played on TV stations around the country. The Bear was always on hand with his zany antics and game picks, which he would print on large cards. When the NCAA banned coaches from appearing on prediction shows, because of several gambling and point-shaving scandals, we went to a panel of celebrity guests.

Through the years, the list included Tom Arnold, Gov. Branstad, Bill Reichardt, Dan Gable, Al McCoy, umpire Tim McClelland, Bump Elliott, Randy Duncan, Kurt Warner and Johnny Orr, to mention just a few.

Babe was one of our favorite guests. One night he fell off the riser and we thought he might be injured. Instead, he jumped right back up and said. "Don't worry. I used to be a boxer. I've taken a few dives in my time." When Keith Murphy joined our staff from Channel 5, he served as part-time producer of the show, and we did some off-the-wall stuff. I came on one time as Elvis and sang "Love Me Tender" with forgettable style.

Occasionally I could be in rare form with my singing. At least Chuck Offenburger thought so. After an appearance on "Beat The Bear", he wrote, "Here's the part I'm never going to forget. Zabel dropped into this mellow baritone voice and began swaying and singing, arms extended, shoulders and head thrown back, as he glided across the studio set, singing like Eddie Cantor did in 1931, 'Another bride, another June, another sunny honeymoon, another season, another reason for makin' WHOOPEE!'" The headline on his 1992 *Register* column read, "After 43 Long Years, Jim Zabel Is Still 'Makin' WHOOPEE!"

Chuck Offenburger liked to hear me sing "Makin' Whoopee"

I later told Chuck my St. Patrick's Day story. I said while I was celebrating in a pub, I got up and sang "When Irish Eyes Are Smiling". A man sitting next to me started to cry. I said "Excuse me sir, are you an Irishman?" He said, "No, I'm a musician."

We did little skits at the beginning of the show involving the Bear. When "The Bridges of Madison County' came out, we got permission to use a scene with Meryl Streep on the air. The truck comes up the driveway, and Meryl Streep walks out on the porch to greet it. But instead of Clint Eastwood in the truck, it's the Bear. He climbs out of the truck, and his card reads, "Where's that damned bridge?" We had a lot of fun with 'Beat the Bear'." It became one of our most popular shows on WHO-TV.

Sundays are a big day for sports. So, why not do a big sports show Sunday night? That's how and why "Two Guys Named Jim" came about. Actually, the idea was suggested by Tim Floyd when he was basketball coach at Iowa State. He loved arena football, and he used to come down and sit in with me when I was broadcasting the Iowa Barnstormers. I did a halftime interview with former ISU football coach Jim Walden during one of our games (he was assisting Barnstormer owner Jim Foster at the time). After the game, Floyd said "You know, you and Walden should do a talk show. You both have a gift of gab."

(The *Des Moines Register* had done a cover story on me in their Sunday edition called "The Talking Machine at Channel 13," and Hayden Fry was once quoted as saying, "When you play Walden, you're already 2,000 words behind by game-time.") The idea clicked. Walden and I have been on the air 13 years as of this writing.

Walden and I actually had taken a few pot-shots at each other through the years when we were talking to our respective fan clubs.

During the "Two Guys Named Jim" show, 2000

Walden asked the Cedar Rapids Cyclone Club, "Do you know what you have when you cross a radio and a microwave? You get four hours of Jim Zabel in 27 minutes. That's about 17 minutes more than you need."

I told the Polk County I-Club "Jim Walden was running off the field after practice the other day and he ran right over a little old lady wearing Cyclone colors. He reached down and picked up the lady, and said "No offense, ma'am." The lady said "No defense either."

The premise of the "Two Jims" show is two guys sitting at a bar talking, and then involving other people in their conversation. The guys are enjoying their libations, but are not drunk. Guys at a bar always seem to open up more than they do in any other environment. And that's what we wanted. Confidential, perceptive, informative stuff. Between the two of us we knew almost every prominent sports personality in Iowa, plus many other coaches and media people around the country. I love interviewing guests, finding out how they feel, what makes them tick. Walden's the same. Plus the fact that he has the coach's expertise and viewpoint, while I have the media approach.

I am often asked about my favorite interview. One of them would have to be Alex Karras. He was (and is) one of the most colorful sports figures I have ever known. An All-American at

Iowa, runner up for the Heisman Trophy, then All-Pro for the Detroit Lions, and after that a major television and movie star and regular on the talk-show circuit. The interview came about after I had called Coach Forest Evashevski to wish him a happy 90th birthday. Evy told me his biggest surprise of the day was that Alex Karras had called him. They had not spoken to each other for 50 years. (Football fans of that era would understand. The feud between coach and player was headline news in its time) So, I called Alex in Los Angeles to ask him what had happened to prompt his change of heart.

He said "Evy is 90, I'm 72. I thought it was time we made our peace." After that, we had a great conversation. Alex admitted he was an impetuous, strong-willed kid when he played at Iowa for an equally strong-willed coach. We talked about the recruiting of Alex. It was like a wild-west show. Everybody wanted him. He was a sensational high school player. Iowa finally hid him out at Lake Okoboji for a month, then signed him. I next talked to Alex in the spring of 2009 on the 35th anniversary of one of my favorite movies, "Blazing Saddles." I asked Alex how he got the role of Mongo. He said "I walked into the office of producer Mel Brooks and dumped all those chains and other things right on his desk, and said "I want the part." Brooks said, "You got it."

Alex still loves the Hawkeyes. So does Walden. Walden wants everyone to know that when others were voting Iowa 6th or 7th on the coaches' poll, he had them No. 1 from the beginning. Is he a closet Hawkeye? No, he's just very perceptive.

Early in my career on WHO-TV, one of our major sponsors, Farm Bureau Insurance, wanted us to televise 11 Sunday games of the Des Moines Triple A baseball team, which then was called the Iowa Oaks and was a farm club of the Oakland A's. So we trotted out our remote truck to the ball park and did the telecasts in living black and white. I hadn't done much baseball, but it was fun and a great play-by-play experience. My analyst, who sat in with me when he wasn't working, was pitcher Vida Blue. He was just 19 then, and had chosen baseball over football. He was an outstanding high school quarterback in Louisiana, but he turned down a scholarship offer from Louisiana State.

One of my favorite interviews was the owner of the Oakland A's, Charles Finley. He made his first millions out of insurance, then became one of the most colorful and successful men in all of baseball. Twins broadcaster Herb Carneal told me that Finley tried to hire him one time. "He flew me to San Francisco and took me out to dinner at Ernie's, one of the fanciest restaurants there. He immediately went into the kitchen. I asked him why, he said "the first thing you do in a good restaurant is tip the chef before the meal". I always remembered that." But he turned down the job. "I felt he might be too tough to work for," Herb said. Harry Caray worked for Finley briefly before he went to Chicago. There's one story about Finley I love to tell. When Catfish Hunter pitched his perfect game for the A's against the Twins in Oakland, Charlie Finley heard the broadcast on his farm in Indiana, Hunter's wife heard it in Louisiana, and his parents heard it in Baltimore. What radio station did they all hear it on? WHO!! We carried Twins baseball for 18 years. (My friends at WCCO in Minneapolis, the originating station for Twins baseball, don't like that story.)

Des Moines is lucky to have a great ballpark and a first-class operational staff headed by general manager Sam Bernabe, one of the best in the country; and an owner, Michael Gartner, who loves and understands the game of baseball.

Chapter 6

THE PERSONALITIES

It's Showtime!

THE FOUR MUSKETEERS
TWO CENTURIES BEHIND THE MIKE

Some of my happiest times, as I look back, were spent with the Four Musketeers—Brooksie, Z, Shoe and Gills. By name, Bob Brooks, Jim Zabel, Ron Gonder and Gene Claussen. (Gonder got the Shoe nickname because he wore size 15, and Claussen was Gills because he always ordered fish when we ate out). For more than 40 years, we traveled together, dined together, stayed in the same hotels together and of course did Hawkeye games together. We were fierce competitors on the air, but best buddies off. (Taking into account our coverage of the Hawkeyes before and after play-by-play, it comes to a total of well over 200 years. My total alone was 65 years, as of May 2009.)

Many times we were joined in our socializing by media friends like Ed Podolak, Buck Turnbull of the *Register*, and George Wine and Phil Haddy of Iowa Sports Information. Our conversations would range from debates and opinions on current games, to individual performances by key players. One time we took an informal poll on Hayden Fry's most valuable player during his 20 years at Iowa. The winner? Reggie Roby! Think of it. What a great feeling it is to know that every kickoff is going into the end zone, every punt is going to travel at least 50 yards, and 50-yard field goals are a given. How valuable is that? As Hayden said of the late Reggie Roby, "he had a leg like a cannon."

Gene Claussen

Sometimes a coach would become involved in our conversations. I remember when Podolak and I were talking with offensive line coach John O'Hara before the 1990 Illinois

HONORING LEGENDS

Jim Zabel   Ron Gonder   Bob Brooks

Iowa's three wisemen

October 19, 2001, Daily Iowan honors 132 years of combined service to the University of Iowa

game in Champaign. The Illini had two of the best defensive ends in the country in Kevin Hardy and Simeon Rice, and they led the Big 10 in total defense. On top of that, this was the first athletic event between the two schools since the much-publicized Bruce Pearl incident involving the recruiting of basketball star Deon Thomas. All of which left Illinois fans furious. O'Hara, who I always felt was one of Iowa's best coaches, had this to say: "I think we'll have some surprises for them." Indeed, the Hawkeyes did. Iowa led 35-7 after the first quarter, and won the game 54-28 for one of the greatest Hawkeye victories ever.

Our "Four Musketeer" evenings usually started this way: Brooksie would say, "CC Manhattan on the rocks, light on the sweet vermouth," Z and Shoe would order Cutty and soda, and Gills would go with a fine wine from his vast personal knowledge of the grape spirit. (He and his wife spent many years traveling to France.) Where to eat? Gills would generally make that decision from the gourmet guide book he carried in his head. We were in Los Angeles for a football game, and Claussen recommended an exclusive restaurant in Beverly Hills called Scandia. It was indeed a fancy place—delicious food, and pricey. I ordered prime rib, Gonder and Claussen had fish, and Brooks ordered the "Viking Sword"—a gourmet spectacular consisting of one lamb chop, one beef tenderloin, and one pork chop all skewered together on a metal spear, which arrived at the table in flames. After extinguishing the blaze, Brooksie wolfed down the meat items with relish. As he was wiping his mouth, a Scandia waiter walked by with a silver tray containing the remaining portion of Beef Wellington he had just served. Brooks immediately snapped to attention. "Waiter!" he shouted. Then again, "Waiter! Could I have some of that Beef Wellington?" The waiter stopped, raised himself up to full stature and then in the most haughty voice I have ever heard he said, "Sir, Scandia does not serve leftovers." So Brooksie was put in his place, but not for long. Someone once said that Brooksie's idea of the perfect meal was sirloin for two for one.

I still have fond memories of our favorite eating places around the Big 10. Let's see how many I can remember. I am doing this from scratch, with no guide except my own memory. There was the Gandy Dancer in Ann Arbor (I loved it when trains came through the depot, and Gonder and I loved it when the smelt were running). There were Charlie's, Harry's, Jimmy's, and more recently, the Blue Horse in Minneapolis (Ray Scott and I used to go to Harry's when we were carrying Twins games); in Columbus, our favorite places were the Jai Lai Club, Morton's and the Columbus Athletic Club (where Woody Hayes used to hold court); in Bloomington, Indiana, there was Little Zagreb with its famous Yugoslavian menu; the spot in West Lafayette where we went before every Purdue game was Seargent Oaks

Phil Haddy and George Wine at the 1985 Rose Bowl

Van Harden digs in

(Wow! What steaks, and Sarge was ready to arm-wrestle any-one who would take him on); if you wanted a great T-bone or porterhouse, the place to go was Smokey's in Madison—before facing the Badgers; in Chicago, the restaurant that Brooksie and Gills always steered us to was the Cape Cod Room at the Drake—great seafood. But the place we all loved the best was The Lark in Tiffin where the Hawkeyes held their press parties for years; Owner Bob Thompson served the famed Lark steak as his signature entrée. Bobby Knight called The Lark the "best steakhouse in the Big 10." Unfortunately, The Lark is only a memory now, it burned to the ground a few years ago.

Brooksie and I had an interesting experience at the Rose Bowl one year. I had interviewed Jack Benny's bandleader, Phil Harris, at Lake Okoboji the previous summer. He and wife Alice Faye were visiting friends there. After the interview, Harris gave me his phone number in Palm Springs and invited me to call him if I got to California. I told Brooks about it and we decided to drive down to Palm Springs since we had an off day covering the Hawkeyes. In Palm Springs, I called Phil Harris's number and Alice Faye answered the phone. She explained that Phil was in Hollywood taping a TV special. She gave me his number.

Brooks and I decided to stay in Palm Springs and eat dinner. We went to a place we had seen advertised as the dining room of

*Jim Zabel with the man in charge,
George Foerstner*

the stars—"Romanoffs on the Rocks." It was a picturesque spot located in the mountain foothills. There was only one catch. There were no stars around. In fact, we were the only two customers in the place. The waiter said, "Frank Sinatra and Dean Martin sit right over there, during the season," as he pointed at a nearby table. The problem was the season didn't start until after the first of the year. Brooks said, "They've got to have a lot of food back there. Let's ask them if we can get a cut rate and unload some of that stuff in the kitchen." No dice. The waiter turned us down. He said he needed all the help he could get until "the season" arrived. I just hope Frank and Dean gave him a big tip.

For years, the Amana VIP golf tournament in Iowa City was the biggest summer sports event in Iowa. Virtually all of the top golfers were there with a bevy of country music stars, sports celebrities like Bobby Knight and Joe DiMaggio, and TV and movie personalities like Glen Campbell and Fred MacMurray. In other words, it was a big deal.

Presiding over the whole affair was George Foerstner, a crusty old German who was the head man at Amana, and later at Raytheon. (George is the guy I called when we were having trouble selling the Bob Commings Coach's Show on WHO-TV. Amana had agreed to buy one-third of the show, so I asked George how to go about selling the remaining two-thirds. "I'll tell you what you do, Zabel," George said in that accent that made him sound like a Prussian general. ("You put your clients in a room, lock the door, then take a damn hatchet to them.") In short, George meant business.

Gonder and I found that out at the VIP media/celebrity party the night before the tournament. After the entertainment that evening, we all retired to a large party room at the motel. The night wore on, and the beverages continued to flow. The crowd gradually dwindled. Finally, the stalwarts who remained there until about 2 a.m. included baseball star Stan Musial, country stars Roy Clark, Charlie Pride and Glen Campbell, and a few media guys like Gonder, myself and Ray Johnson, a WHO-TV sales executive who came with me. Roy Clark, who had a 7 a.m. tee-off time, continued to perform for us, as did Charlie Pride, and we kept egging them on. And so it went. It was actually a memorable evening and the country stars and Stan Musial were great. But the repercussions were about ready to start. A letter of reprimand from George Foerstner came to Gonder's boss at WMT, and my boss, Bob Harter, also got a critical letter about me. Even Bump Elliott received notification to take more control of "his people."

But the real bombshell took place six weeks later. Roy Clark appeared on Johnny Carson, and the first thing he did was

With Hayden Fry and Steve Shannon

apologize for missing a scheduled guest shot on the Carson show several weeks earlier. Clark said, "I was at a golf tournament in Iowa, and after a late night of entertainment, and trying to make a 7 a.m. tee-off, I came down with pneumonia. And it was bad." Roy looked a little thin and pale. The VIP underwent some changes too. The media had their own party, separate from the contestants and celebrities. It wasn't quite the same. None of us can sing and play the guitar.

The "Four Musketeers" ended their play-by-play days when Iowa went exclusive. It was a great run while it lasted. I feel that collectively we gave fans the most complete coverage of Iowa football they have ever had. I know that I personally received over twelve-hundred cards and letters when the change took place. I feel that Podolak and I fit well together as a broadcast team. Podolak is a superb analyst, the best around. I knew that when I hired him. He also has nine lives. A few years after he started working with me, a newly-hired executive who I knew was a "cost-cutter" took me to lunch at the Des Moines Club. I knew he wanted something. Shortly after the salad course, he said to me, "Do you realize what we're paying Ed Podolak?" I said I did. He said, "That's more than the Bears pay Dick Butkus." I replied, "That's because he's better than Dick Butkus." He then tried to placate me and asked, "Would you be willing to take so-and-so from your sports department as your color man?" (He's no longer there, and the guy he referred to couldn't ad lib sleep after drinking Ovaltine). I said, "No." I added, and these are my exact words, "If Podolak leaves, I leave." End of conversation.

Podolak put another of those nine lives on the line early in 2009 when he was accused of some unbecoming behavior and imbibing too much following Iowa's bowl game in Florida. Iowa threatened to fire Podolak from the broadcast team, and Podolak threatened to resign. Eddie was miffed, and Iowa was mad. I got on the phone with Eddie, who was playing golf with Willie Nelson in San Francisco. I told him he needed Iowa, Iowa needed him, that the fans loved him, but he needed to

Hawkeye Broadcast Buddies: (back) Bob Brooks, Gary Dolphin, Jim Zabel (front) Ed Podolak, Ron Gonder

straighten up his personal life. I told him, "You cannot leave the broadcast. I'll kill you."

Then I called Gary Dolphin and Randy Peterson and got them on our Sunday night show "Two Guys Named Jim," and they did a great job in Podolak's defense. Next, I got my boss Joel McCrea and my buddy Dale Howard involved with Iowa A.D. Gary Barta. I also want to thank Coach Kirk Ferentz for calling Eddie, and associate athletic director Rick Klatt for hiring Eddie in the first place when Iowa went exclusive. It was a great move.

How do the Four Musketeers feel today? Gene Claussen of course is gone and we miss him. The rest of us are still closely connected to the Hawkeyes. Brooksie attends all the games, does radio reports, and has a sports show on Mediacom. Of course, I am still gainfully employed by WHO, thanks to Joel McCrea and Van Harden who happens to be one of the most brilliant program directors anywhere. I love doing "Two Jims" with Jim Walden, "Sound-Off" with Jon Miller, the Wednesday

"Hawkeye Nation" show with Joe Chmelka's I-Club Group. I told Brooksie, "We're not doing too bad for two guys who started out doing chariot races." (I think Brooksie actually knew Ben Hur.) Talking about our WHO Hawkeye football network, it wouldn't have been possible without Sally Robson. She was a great manager. Steve Shannon deserves similar praise. He was an early benefactor at WHO.

Ron Gonder, the third surviving member of the Four Muske- teers, is completely content. He does regular reports on WMT, and he is always kind enough to send me a copy, and he and his wife Pat lead travel tours around the world.

Do we miss doing play-by-play? Of course. It gets in your blood. You love the challenge, the excitement, the color and thrill of game day. In my own case, I will have to admit I enjoyed doing arena football for seven years. I did all of Kurt Warner's games. And, frankly, it satisfied my thirst for play-by-play. Now I can listen to and watch the Hawkeyes without having to battle the crowds, the weather, and the traffic jams.

So, go Gary! Go Ed! Go Hawks! And go Four Musketeers.

We love it! We love it! We love it!

Halftime awards for Gonder, Zabel and Brooks

Photo printed with permission by the Des Moines Register

DUTCH & JFK: PRESIDENTIAL REMINISCING

I interviewed Ronald Reagan 18 times, at all stages of his career, including the White House. One interview that I vividly remember took place when Reagan returned to Des Moines to promote a movie he had made with Piper Laurie. He was about 40, newly divorced from Jane Wyman and newly elected president of the Screen Actors Guild.

As his parade came down Walnut Street, I got him out of his convertible and into our studios at 914 Walnut. We went into the studio where Reagan had once done his sportscasts and Chicago Cubs ticker tape broadcasts, and we started our interview. We talked about his days at WHO, his broadcasts of Iowa sootball games, his life in Hollywood (he was palling around with guys like Errol Flynn and Jimmy Stewart) his views on TV play-by-play sports broadcasts (he was against exclusivity because he thought it made announcers lazy and deprived fans of complete and diverse coverage).

Ronald Reagan

We talked and talked and finally I said, "Well, Dutch I guess we better end the interview because we've talked so long the station may want to hire you back, and I'll be out of a job." Reagan said, "That's all right, Jim. You stay out of Hollywood and I'll stay out of Des Moines."

After the interview we went into the program director's office (Harold Fair) and had a couple of beers. Then Reagan left to call friends he wanted to visit. While he was gone, I asked his agent who was with him, how Reagan had made it so big in Hollywood. The agent said "three reasons: he's always on time, he always knows his lines, and he never argues with the director. And then—there's that smile."

Ah yes, "that smile." I saw a lot of it that night as we visited Reagan's friends around Des Moines, many of whom were present and former WHO employees. Amid much laughter (and occasional sitting on laps) Reagan talked about taking horseback riding lessons at the Fort Des Moines Army Post, swimming in the huge Camp Dodge pool (he was a former lifeguard), acting at the Des Moines Community Playhouse, broadcasting Hawkeye games, and the crazy parties they had back in the 1930s (near beer and alcohol was the favorite Prohibition beverage).

I said to Reagan during the course of the evening, "It sounds like you had a lot of fun while you were here." Reagan replied, "It was the happiest time of my life. And why not? I was young, I had a yellow convertible, and I was doing what I loved—broadcasting sports." There was no talk of politics that night.

Fast forward 30 years. I went to the White House in 1981 to interview President Reagan on the event of our 50th year of broadcasting Iowa Football, and to celebrate the fact the Hawkeyes were going to the Rose Bowl.

I was set up in a communications room adjoining the Oval Office. Reagan had made a major foreign policy speech that morning, and when he came into the room he was surrounded by advisers. I could hear the President asking "What did London say? How about Paris? That's what I expected from Moscow." About that time Reagan spotted the WHO logo on my microphone. He walked over, we shook hands and he said, "How about those Hawkeyes?" I said we were as proud of Iowa going to the Rose Bowl as we were of a President of the United States being one of the first to broadcast Hawkeye games. Then we launched into the interview, and even though I called him Mr. President at first, we soon became "Dutch and Jim," two

Top left: Reagan started off as a lifeguard
Top right: Dutch and dog during WHO days
Bottom: Jim and Dutch at the mike

Celebrating WHO's 50th Anniversary

sportscasters talking about the big games and other thrilling moments at the microphone.

Reagan was a great interview and had many fond memories of WHO and Des Moines. We ran the interview on both WHO radio and WHO-TV. After my visit to the White House, I thought about all the TV and radio stations, and newspapers that had called me after Reagan was elected president, wanting to know if I had any recordings of his play-by-play, and also wanting to know what he "was really like."

The *Chicago Tribune, L.A. Times, Miami Herald* and *San Francisco Chronicle* were some of the newspapers that called. My answer to all of them was that the powerful Musicians Union did not allow any recordings or transcriptions to be made during the 1930s for fear they would drive live musicians out of business. Of course the ban was aimed at musical performers, but it also applied to broadcasters. The only thing I had was some simulated play-by-play Reagan did in describing how he got his job at WHO. I also described Reagan as a man with a lot of talent and a high degree of "likeability." You just wanted to be around him. That was always Reagan's strength. And then— there was that smile.

I interviewed Senator John F. Kennedy at halftime of the Iowa-Notre Dame game in 1958, when he was a candidate for the Democratic nomination for president. As reported in an earlier chapter, Iowa was leading by two touchdowns at the half, I said, "Senator Kennedy, what do you think of the game?" He replied, "I'm pulling for Iowa and praying for Notre Dame." A ready-made politician, right?

A tragic post-script to the Iowa-Notre Dame series was written in 1963. That year's game, scheduled for Nov. 23, was canceled because of President Kennedy's assassination.

Back in the 1950s, I was assigned to cover the opening of the Hoover Library at West Branch. Our newsroom didn't have anyone to send when NBC called requesting coverage, so Jack Shelley asked me , since that part of the state was my regular sports beat. President Hoover was there, of course, along with Presidents Truman and Eisenhower. When I interviewed President Hoover, I can still remember him standing on the porch of his tiny home, then pointing across the road and saying "right over there, in that field, I used to pick potato bugs for 10 cents an hour." Although Hoover has been largely—and perhaps wrongfully—blamed for the Great Depression, he was a highly intelligent man and a joy to interview. I could not help but think what a vital part of American history these three presidents had witnessed.

Richard Nixon came to our studios on two occasions, and I interviewed him both times. He was glib to the point of being a little too slick, I felt. I also interviewed Jimmy Carter at our studios, and later his wife Rosalynn and Jane Fonda, who was probably the most controversial woman in America at that time.

I talked with President Clinton when he was touring our station during the floods, and I reminded him he was standing next to a portrait of Ronald Reagan. He got a kick out of that.

My first political assignment in my early days at WHO was covering Gov. Thomas E. Dewey when he ran against Truman. He was confident to the point of arrogance. It was that confidence that led to the *Chicago Tribune*'s famously erroneous headline "Dewey Defeats Truman." Truman, of course, was the actual winner, and to this day many believe it was Truman's last-minute speech to the 100,000 people attending the WHO Plowing Matches at Dexter that swung the election in his favor. Such is the power of the Voice of the Middle West!

Other Notable Interviews Along the Way

Above: With Tom Watson, world champion golfer

Below: Andy North and Nancy Lopez

BRIGHT LIGHTS & STARDUST: THE CELEBRITY BEAT

What do Bob Hope, Bill Cosby, Michael Jordan, Amy Vanderbilt, Rocky Marciano, Sinclair Lewis, Duncan Hines, Mary Pickford, Gloria Swanson, and Lady Astor have in common?

Very little—except in my mind and memory. They gave me some moments I will never forget.

When the State Fair called and asked me to introduce Bob Hope at his Grandstand show, I was flattered and awed. Hope was a hero! Here was a man who dominated the entire entertainment spectrum for generations—vaudeville, radio, TV, movies—Hope was No. 1 in all. Then there were the annual tours overseas at Christmas time to entertain the troops, and his personal appearances as well.

The first time I ever interviewed Bob Hope was at halftime of an Iowa football game at the Coliseum in Los Angeles. He came on with actor Don DeFore (a native Iowan), and when I asked Hope about his investment in the Cleveland Indians baseball team (in those days a perennial loser), he replied, "Ah yes, Cleveland—that small town just outside the American League." I actually first saw Hope in person at a Bond Rally in downtown Des Moines in the 1950s. His opening line then was: "I want to thank the mayor for presenting me with this key—to the bus station washroom."

The main thing about introducing Hope is that I got to spend a full day with him, or at least most of one.

I met him at the orchestra rehearsal in the Grand Ballroom of the Fort Des Moines Hotel, and watched as he and his wife, Dolores, ran through their musical numbers. Then, that night, I joined him at 6:30 in his dressing room behind the big stage at the fair. He could not have been more charming. He was fascinated when I pointed to the green "judges' stand" nearby, where I called many a Saturday night stock car race on the Fairgrounds track.

"Back in the 1930s," I said, "Dutch Reagan announced the races from right up there." Hope idolized Reagan, and could not get over the fact that the President of the United States stood right on that very platform to do auto races back in the days of Barney Oldfield. Hope reminisced about his days on Broadway—he was a major star there in the 1930s. "In 1933," he said, "I was in the musical 'Roberta' with Fred Astaire and his sister, Adele, and would you believe, down in the orchestra pit were Benny Goodman, Glenn Miller, Artie Shaw, and Tommy Dorsey, all young musicians then." Five years later, or course, they all had their own orchestras—and were a major part of the Big Band Era.

After talking with Hope and his wife for more than an hour, his musical director came in and said to me: "We will have a 20-second doughnut inside the theme for your introduction." My God! I thought—20-<u>seconds</u>! I've got 20 <u>minutes</u> worth of material! But a short time later, with the strains of "Thanks for the Memories" as background, I came out on the stage in front of a crowd of close to 20,000 people, and said something like, "Now, ladies and gentlemen, to the man who has given us so many memories, we give our thanks—Bob Hope."

Hope was in rare form. People who have not seen him do a show without cue cards, such as in his old vaudeville days, cannot believe what a great, natural stand-up comic he was.

(One of my favorites was the story about the young man going to confession in Ireland. He said, "Father, I have committed adultery." The priest said, "I cannot grant you absolution, my son, unless I know the name of the other party." "I cannot tell you that, Father. I have been sworn to secrecy." The priest then said, "Was it Miss Connolly, the new young teacher down in the village?" "No, it wasn't her," the young man answered. "Was it the Widow O'Sullivan?" the priest inquired. "No, it wasn't her," the young man replied. "Well, then, was it Mrs. O'Flahrety, who has been known to flaunt herself about the village?" "No, it wasn't her either," the young man answered. The priest became irate and said, "I am afraid I cannot grant you absolution. You will have to say your beads 50 times." The young man left the church and met his buddy waiting outside. "Well, what happened?" he asked. "Did he grant you absolution?" "No," the young man said. "But he gave me three pretty good leads.")

After the show, I asked Hope if I could record an interview with him. He said I could talk with him while he walked his dog that night. So, there we were, the two of us and the dog, at 2 a.m., walking down by the railroad tracks south of the Fort Des Moines Hotel, with me asking questions about his life and times and what was Bing Crosby "really like?" A night to remember.

Bill Cosby has had at least three major careers in his lifetime, stretching all the way from his comedy club days to his TV dominance of the 90s. Back in the 1970s, he was one of NBC's major stars, and he came to Des Moines for a personal appearance. Part of his network agreement was that he would cut promotional spots for the local NBC station of whatever town he was in. So, here he was at WHO-TV doing everything we asked him to do. Finally, he asked, "Where's your sports guy?" So, I trotted out and told him that I did Iowa football—which at that time was in the midst of one of its worst seasons on record. I did not tell him that Iowa had just been beaten by Michigan, 55-0. I asked Cosby, who was wearing army fatigues, what the premise of the spot would be. He said, "I'll be sitting on a park bench reading a newspaper, and you come by and say, 'I wonder who this bum is?'" So, I did exactly that. When I said, "I wonder who this bum is?" Cosby lowered the newspaper so I could see him there smoking his trademark cigar. "Bill Cosby!" I shouted. "What are you doing here? You're a famous TV star!" "Yes, I was," he replied very dejectedly, "but I lost all my money betting on Iowa football." Then, as an afterthought—"I thought I had it made last week. I had Iowa and 54½ points against Michigan." (Remember, I hadn't told him told him about the Michigan game. The man was perceptive.)

With George Raveling

In 1984, the U.S. Olympic team was playing an exhibition game in Phoenix, and I ran into my buddy, George Raveling (assistant Olympic coach), who was on a shopping spree in Biltmore Fashion Park, one of the high-tone malls—which happened to be having a major sale that day. George was a non-stop shopper. With him that day was the star player on that team, Michael Jordan. We talked and joked, and Jordan agreed to come on George's coaches' show later that year, on WHO radio, and which I hosted.

When the moment arrived the following winter, I asked Jordan, on the air, "How do you get along with George? What has he taught you?"

With mock seriousness, Jordan replied, "He said he was going to teach me how to dress, and I look like a bum. He said he was going to teach me how to get along with girls, and I can't get a date. And he said he was going to help me invest my money, and I don't have a dime to my name."

George replied, "The kid's a slow learner. But he's not a bad basketball player."

I was interviewing Amy Vanderbilt about her latest, best-selling book on etiquette. Before we started, she cautioned me, "Please don't ask me if I have been to Des Moines before." After the interview, I said, "Why?" Then she explained. "I was a lobbyist for Swift & Company during the legislative battle over oleomargarine a few years ago." This was one of the most divisive issues ever to come before the State Legislature—the dairy interests vs. the big-time margarine producers. I always felt it was a little incongruous—this lady who made her fame and fortune telling readers about proper table settings and formal wedding invitations, being involved in a knock-down battle over farm products in the state of Iowa.

Lady Astor, the renowned and controversial British society leader, was in town to appear before the Des Moines Women's Club. It was one of the major civic and social events of the season. Naturally, during an interview with her, I had to ask about one of the most celebrated controversies of that time—her much-publicized feud with playwright George Bernard Shaw (which was in the news again because of the success of "My Fair Lady," which was based on his original play, "Pygmalion")

"It's true," she said with that definitive English accent, "We hated each other."

She confessed she did try to make up to him one time by inviting him to tea. Her formal invitation read: "Lady Astor will be at home, Tuesday, April 16, at 4 p.m."

Shaw replied on his RSVP Note: "So will George Bernard Shaw."

When I was editor-in-chief of *The Daily Iowan* during my college days in Iowa City, I interviewed the famed playwright William Saroyan, who had just won the Pulitzer Prize for his Broadway play, "The Time of Your Life," which starred Gene

Jim Zabel and Bob Quinn celebrate their birthdays together at WHO—121 years total

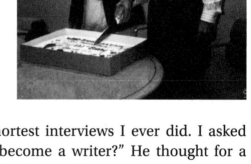

Kelly. It was one the shortest interviews I ever did. I asked Saroyan, "How do you become a writer?" He thought for a moment, then replied, "Read everything you can until you're 21, then write like hell."

That is easier to say than to accomplish. When I later interviewed Sinclair Lewis, the renowned author of such prize-winning works as "Main Street" and "Dodsworth" he said the hardest thing for young writers to do was to "get to the typewriter." Lewis taught for several years at the Sorbonne in Paris. "This was during the glory years of Hemingway and F. Scott Fitzgerald, but for most of the would-be authors it was a case of 'talk, talk, and talk'—and no production. Writing is hard work. You just have to sit down and do it. It requires energy and discipline. For most of them, I think, the big thing was fear—they were afraid that what they put down on paper would not be good enough—whereas they could go on talking and pretending forever, as long as the money held out."

Lewis was remarkably candid about his own work. I recall going into a campus bookstore with him, where he was supposed to autograph copies of his latest novel, *Elmer Gantry*.

"Don't buy it," he told the young lady. "I'm not very proud of it." The book, or course, later became a successful movie and a star-vehicle for Burt Lancaster.

Lewis dismissed his own legendary status as one of the greatest writers of his generation. "I was just a kid from a small Minnesota town who wrote about the things and the people he knew and saw everyday."

For his style of biographical novel, he did it as well as anyone has ever done.

DUNCAN HINES
SOME HOME COOKIN'

Statistical Note of Interest: The Des Moines Public Library once told me they had more copies of my *Jim Zabel's Fabulous Pink Apron Cookbook* (37) than they did of Julia Child's.

Which leads me into my interview with another giant of the culinary world, Duncan Hines. Everyone knows him as the "Cake Mix King", but he also prided himself on being a gourmet chef.

His appearance bore out his obvious interest in food, and lots of it. He admitted his favorite breakfast was "corn flakes with ice cream" when I interviewed him. He was jovial and spoke with great gusto in a broad Southern accent.

After talking eloquently about his cake mixes and other pastries, he described life on his "plantation" in Tennessee. That's where the corn flakes and ice cream came up. As a final question, I asked him how he prepared a steak, which most Americans consider to be the ultimate dinner.

"First of all," he said, "I don't just buy prime beef from a butcher shop. I buy <u>prize</u> beef from the Chicago stockyards—the very best. I have them cut it four inches thick, then fly it to my plantation in Tennessee. I sear the meat on both sides over a hot fire to seal in the juices. Then I cook it the rest of the way over green hickory logs, which provide a maximum of smoke and flavor."

By this time, Hines' face was florid, and he was practically drooling with his description. He was carried away with rapture. So was I.

"Is it good?" I asked intently.

"Oh God Man!" came the fervent reply. It's the first time I ever heard a steak described with the passion of a love affair.

ROCKY MARCIANO SIDEWALK JUSTICE

As an interviewer, there is always that certain question you want to ask a specific person. I wanted to ask a heavyweight boxing champion if anyone beat him up as a kid. Sounds silly, but it was true.

My opportunity came when I saw Rocky Marciano walk into the studio. He was in town to promote the Golden Gloves Tournament.

We talked about the boxing game, which I had grown up with – Sugar Ray Robinson, Joe Louis, Muhammad Ali, and, of course, Marciano's own career.

Finally, at the end, I asked my question—"Did anybody beat you up when you were a kid?"

Marciano looked startled. "Nobody's ever asked me that question," he said. "And I've been interviewed a thousand times." He thought for a moment, then said, "Yeah, there was this guy in my neighborhood about three years older than me. I was 13 and he was around 16 or 17. He'd pick on me every chance he got, and then one day he beat me so bad my mother had to call the doctor."

"What happened then?" I asked.

"The kid moved away," Rocky said. "But he came back about four years later, and I ran into him. I was about 50 pounds heavier and I had taken up boxing. The guy said, "I don't remember you. Who are you?" So I introduced myself. First, with one fist to the jaw, then one to the stomach, and another to the jaw as he was falling down. I never saw the guy again, and I don't think he wanted to see me."

SILVER SCREEN SIRENS

Mary Pickford was called "America's Sweetheart" during her heyday in early Hollywood. She was the top star of her time and was also an astute business woman. Along with her husband, Douglas Fairbanks, she helped to found United Artists Studio with partners Charlie Chaplin and famed director D.W. Griffith. Her home, Pickfair, was the best known movie star address in Hollywood.

Naturally, it was a big item that she was in Des Moines to speak to the Women's Club. The media was invited to interview her in the Presidential Suite of the Savery Hotel. I set up my recorder and did my interview with the petite star (she stood 4-11). We talked about the Golden Era of Hollywood compared to the present day, and what her greatest moments were. I went back to the station with my interview and found, much to my dismay, there was nothing on the tape (this was in the early days of recorders).

I called Pickford's manager, explained my plight, and asked for another time to do the interview. He was strangely hesitant at first, but finally agreed to 3 p.m., after Pickford returned from her speech. When I entered the Presidential Suite, I knew something was wrong. What I didn't know, but found out later, was that Pickford was a chronic alcoholic who drank a quart of bourbon a day. She was giddy as I set up my recorder and became flirtatious as we started the interview. It got worse from there. She put her hand on my knee and invited me to move to Pickfair. I tried to play the whole thing as a joke, and said, "but you're already married—what would your husband think?" (Her current husband was bandleader Buddy Rogers.) She replied, "Buddy loves company. You simply have to come to Pickfair—I want you to." Somehow, someway I got through the interview, and despite some slurred words, got enough of an interview to put on the air. I thought to myself, "Now I know why they call her America's Sweetheart."

Gloria Swanson was another Hollywood movie legend who came to town. She won an Academy Award for her portrayal of fading screen star Norma Desmond, in "Sunset Boulevard". She was in Des Moines to publicize the release of the picture. She was also very petite (she stood barely 5 feet tall), but was as definitive as the on-screen Norma when she spoke. I asked her what differentiates the great stars of yesteryear from those of today. "We had faces!" she said with authority, emphasizing the word "faces". "That's why we made such beautiful films." Then I asked, "Is it true you were the highest-paid star in Hollywood?"

"Yes," came the answer.

"How much did you make?"

"Ten thousand dollars a week" she replied, "and I spent every dime of it."

(My God, I thought—there was no income tax, pork chops were six cents a pound during the Depression, gas was 13 cents a gallon, theater admissions were 25 cents.)

"How could you possibly do that?" I asked.

"We would have parties with 400 guests," she said, "and as favors we would give each one a solid gold cigarette lighter. Then there were mansions, and limousines, and trips to Paris... and there were divorces. We were stars, and we lived like stars!"

So if you want to know what old time Hollywood was really like, watch "Sunset Boulevard" on Turner Classic Movies, or visit with Norma.

DUNCAN VS. REICHARDT
FAST FRIENDS—FURIOUS FOES

When it comes to stop-at-nothing, burn-the-house-down competition, I am willing to give some credence to the Red Sox against the Yankees, Michigan vs. Ohio State, Kobe against LeBron or Tom Brands against the World, but none of them compares to Randy Duncan against Bill Reichardt. Theirs was a confrontation for the ages.

Both of them have their names etched eternally in the Hawkeye Book of Mythology. Duncan was runner up for the Heisman; he played in two winning Rose Bowl Games, and the 1958 Iowa team that he quarterbacked is considered by many to be Iowa's greatest.

Reichardt was a bulldozing fullback at Iowa, a superstar who did something no other Big 10 Conference player has ever done—He was named MVP of the Big 10 from a team that did not win a Big 10 game.

They were as close as two friends could ever be, but their rivalry was just as intense as their camaraderie.

The dust still hasn't settled on the tennis courts at Okoboji, or the handball courts at the Des Moines YMCA where their legendary encounters took place. Observers still marvel at the ferocity of the competition. A few golf courses also felt their vengeance, although neither could sink a 5-foot putt.

But their most tenacious exchanges played out verbally.

"Duncan," Reichardt said, "You inherited your father's law practice, you live in your father-in-law's house in Des Moines, and in your wife's home at the lake—Have you ever done anything for yourself?"

The two were at a party when Reichardt was in the legislature. During the course of the evening, a nice little old lady came

Randy Duncan vs. Bill Reichardt

up to Duncan, mistakenly thinking he was Reichardt. "Oh, Mr. Reichardt," she said, "I want to thank you for what you are doing in the legislature." Duncan replied, "It's none of your business what I'm doing in the legislature". "Well!" she huffed, "That's the last time you'll get my vote!"

Both were dining at one of Des Moines' most prestigious private clubs, when Randy told a few off-color stories. Reichardt obtained a sheet of the club's stationery, and had his secretary type a formal letter to Duncan, stating that "many people were offended" by his joke-telling, and had complained to the management. "The Board of Directors held an emergency meeting, "the letter read "and voted to expel you from the club." Signed by the manager.

Duncan called Reichardt in a state of panic. "I'm in real trouble now," he said, and then read the letter. Reichardt consoled him and let him stew for a while before he admitted the ruse.

They constantly ridiculed each other's playing ability. Reichardt said, "Duncan was so slow my grandmother could catch him, and she has a bad leg."

Randy said, "Reichardt played when there were leather helmets, 50 cent admissions, and fullbacks didn't have to block, because he never did."

I was doing "Beat the Bear" with the two of them on WHO-TV. Randy had me get together with the film people in Iowa City

Tom Brands: "Tomorrow the world, then Reichardt and Duncan next!

and pick out plays from Reichardt's games where he was <u>not</u> carrying the football. We found some where he was just standing there, sometimes hopping up and down, but never blocking. We ran the film on "Beat the Bear." It was hilarious. Cruel? Yes, but that was the nature of their humor. Reichardt, for the first time, was speechless. Randy said, "No wonder those other Iowa backs all walk with canes today."

Reichardt's clothing business often entered the fray. "I give Duncan all of my old suits," Reichardt said, "I just have to take in the shoulders and let out the waist." Duncan said, "Reichardt's customers always come back. The reason is the buttons start falling off after a month."

At various times, both Randy and Bill served as my color analyst on our Iowa football broadcasts. Randy had a mind of his own in the broadcast booth. One time, after Iowa's flamboyant young quarterback, Matt Szykowny, had turned in a spectacular performance in leading the Hawkeyes to victory, I sent Randy to the locker room to get some player interviews. When he came back, I asked him "Did you get Szykowny?" Randy said, "No." I said, "Why? He was the star of the game!" Randy said, "I don't like him!"

On another occasion, I was describing Hawkeye quarterback Gary Snook going back to pass, but after looking downfield for a potential receiver, I realized that Snook had not thrown the ball at all, and that is what I said. Duncan broke in. "What happened," he said, "is that Snook threw the ball, but a defensive lineman batted it back at him and he caught it."

"Just like Terry Hanratty at Notre Dame," I said.

Jim and Bill in the broadcast booth

"Yeah," Randy answered, "you <u>saw</u> that one."

Randy also worked with me on our nightly 6:15 sports show on WHO-TV. One night we had basketball star Denise Long as our guest. She was well over 6-feet tall, and towered over Randy when we sat down for the rehearsal. Randy ran out of the studio before the show and came back with three Des Moines telephone directories to sit on. He said, "No high school girl is going to be taller than me when I'm sitting down."

Bill also had his eccentricities. He had a well-publicized feud with Forest Evashevski, and refused to go to Iowa games when Evy was Athletic Director. Finally, I convinced him to make his peace and come on with me for a halftime interview at the Iowa-Michigan game. He showed up, we did a long interview and I thought that everything was peaches-and-cream again with Bill and Hawkeye football. I later discovered that he had driven to Iowa City, just in time for the interview, then got back in his car and drove back to Des Moines, without seeing any of the game.

Bill had definite ideas on everything. I asked him one time if he was going up to Lake Okoboji for July 4th. He said, "Hell, I don't like those people down here. Why should I go up there to see them?"

As Don Rickles once said, "Insult is the highest form of flattery."

Bill called me once in Scottsdale and wanted to take me to lunch. "I've got something to show you," he said enthusiastically. What he had was a copy of the All-Time 100-Year Iowa Football Team; just released.

Reichardt was first-team fullback. Duncan was on the second team. Bill could not suppress his jubilation. "Duncan says he's going to demand a recount," Reichardt laughed.

Underneath, Bill was really a caring, warm-hearted person. He was colorful and controversial. He made good copy. The late Rob Borsellino did some great columns on him in the *Register*. He was involved in politics and causes of all kinds. He was a true personality in every sense of the word. Every time I see his widow, Sue, I am reminded of how much we miss him and all those marvelous confrontations with Randy Duncan.

I called Bill in the hospital shortly before he passed away. Sue was there, as were his children, Duke, Doug and Barb. Also, Borsellino and Randy. Bill and I talked just briefly. Later, he asked Randy, "Duncan, am I dying?" It was the toughest question he ever tried to answer from Bill.

Bill and Randy—a sight for sore eyes

DANCING WITH THE STAR: CLORIS AND ME

Artie Shaw was playing at the Tromar and I needed a date. I was new to Des Moines, but my best friend was Neal Ashby, son of *Des Moines Tribune* Columnist Ted Ashby, and he knew practically everybody. His girlfriend, Jody, knew even more. She recommended a friend of hers named Cloris Leachman, a recent graduate of Roosevelt High School, and already a rising star at the Des Moines Community Playhouse. "She's perfect for you," Jody said, "She's a pistol." Indeed. And a dead shot. She was good-looking and vivacious, with a personality that came on you like July 4th fireworks. (She went on in her long career to play women like Grandma Moses, but remember when she was 19 she was a runner-up in the Miss America contest.)

So Cloris and I went to the Tromar, located then at 6th and Keo, to dance to the music of Artie Shaw. She was a good dancer, and I wasn't too bad myself, although no threat to Fred Astaire. Cloris and I hit it off. We dated off and on most of my first summer in Des Moines. I didn't have a car (you couldn't buy one during the war), but we made do with cabs, street cars, walking, and finding appropriate places to go. After all, it was summer and we were young. Come fall we parted ways. Cloris went off to college at Northwestern in Evanston.

The rest of the story comes from my sister, Joan. She belonged to the Pi Phi sorority at Northwestern. Cloris went through rush, and at the Pi Phi house she met my sister. Cloris said, "Zabel, that's an unusual name. Do you know Jim Zabel in Des Moines?" Joan said, "He's my brother." Cloris then unfolded the story of our romantic summer, in some detail. The Pi Phis blackballed her then and there immediately. Years later, I interviewed Cloris in Des Moines and she laughed about the incident. "They kicked me out of the damn house," she said, "and I hadn't even gotten to the best part." The best part actually came with dozens of movies and TV shows, Academy Awards, record appearances on "Dancing with the Stars" and the honor of being Grand Marshal of The Tournament of Roses Parade. I'd say the Pi Phis were the losers.

CAFFERTY IS.......
AN IRREPRESSIBLE MAVERICK

What can I tell you about Jack Cafferty that you don't already know?

Plenty!

I worked with him for several years on our WHO-TV newscasts at 6 and 10 p.m. He was a tall, good-looking Irishman with a movie-star smile, split second wit, a tenacious work ethic and a will to succeed like tempered steel.

I considered Jack one of my closest friends, but on the air we were competitive and occasionally even combative. I prided myself on being pretty adept at one-liners, but Jack was just about impossible to top.

One night I came on with a story about Olympic champion Nadia Comaneci and an honor she had just won.

Jack asked, "What's new in sports Mr. Zabel?"

I replied, "Nadia Comaneci was named Woman of The Year by the Associated Breast."

Jack said, "You really know a lot about gymnastics, don't you?"

I said, "I used to be an expert on the parallel bars."

Jack replied, "You mean those bars on opposite sides of the street," gesturing with his arms as he spoke.

The other two members of our news panel were Jerry Reno and Phil Thomas, both solid TV personalities. (I always felt we were a good combo. We had a lot of chemistry and we got some of the best news ratings WHO-TV has ever had. In fact, for the first and only time we drew even with Russ VanDyke on Channel 8).

If you read Jack's two books, you know he was raised in Las Vegas, his father was married eight times, and by his own

WHO-TV13 News, 1977: (left to right) Jerry Reno, Jack Cafferty, Phil Thomas, and Jim Zabel

admission he had a drinking problem. Honestly, as close as I was to Jack and as much time as we spent together, I never saw that in him. He was all business at work, and a whirlwind of activity off the set, investing in apartment buildings and other financial ventures.

Jack came to WHO-TV from Kansas City, where he was a TV weatherman.

He is a scratch golfer and loves the game. In Kansas City, he played with golfing great Tom Watson. (Every time I covered the Amana VIP Golf Tournament in Iowa City, Tom would ask me about "Cafferty.") Jack later caddied for Jack Nicklaus in an 18-hole exhibition at Wakonda Club. We filmed the entire match and carried it on WHO-TV.

Jack was a dynamo at work. He made a lot of changes in our TV news department which rankled one particular front-office executive who Jack didn't like anyway. "The guy doesn't know anything about TV news," Jack said. "He doesn't belong there." The man in question was later fired.

One of Jack's more interesting decisions was to hire veteran newspaperman George Mills, who had just retired from the *Des Moines Register*. "Lefty," as he was known from his softball days, was already in his early 70s. I remember a newsroom staff meeting shortly after that. Jack was wondering how to cover the anniversary of the famed "March on the Statehouse", which took place in 1933. "Maybe we should check the library files," Jack said. "You don't have to do that," George advised. "I was there in 1933. I covered the story for the *Register*."

George proved to be invaluable, particularly in his coverage of historical stories, which Iowa seems to have a lot of.

I have often said that the best local television ever done in Des Moines was a series called "Cafferty Is..." Jack was a ballerina, a bartender at Babe's, a harness racer at the Fairgrounds, a tank commander at Camp Dodge, a hair stylist and a number of other intriguing professional people. The series was a smash hit. Jack is a great ad-libber with a cynical sense of humor. (All of which have served him well on his rise to stardom in New York.) That brings me to the inevitable fact I had realized for a long time—Jack was destined for bigger things. He kept me posted. Philadelphia was interested in him. But before he could pursue that job, New York came calling. I got the news one Sunday night when I ran into Jack and his wife Carol at the movies. It was the news I really didn't want to hear but knew that I would. "It's New York," Jack said. "NBC wants me for 'Live at Five.' " So, that was it. The Cafferty era was over in Des Moines, and just beginning in New York.

Jack Cafferty had an immediate impact on New York. You may recall his comment which made national headlines at the time. (This was a few years ago when purity ruled the airwaves on TV. You may remember that Jack Paar was taken off the air in the fifties for using the phrase "water closet" in referring to a toilet). Cafferty said "The weather sucks" in New York. He was still that irrepressible scamp. *New York* magazine did a cover story on him, and he became the talk of the town.

I visited Jack several times when he was at NBC. Bob Hope was his guest one night, sportscaster Marv Albert came by, and David Letterman strolled in from an adjacent studio where he was taping his show. Jack took it all in stride. Afterward we went to Jack and Carol's home in New Jersey and out to eat.

When our youngest daughter, Diane, graduated we took her on an extended visit to New York and Washington. The highlight of the trip was our visit with Jack and Carol. Jack got us tickets to "Saturday Night Live." So we saw the original cast— John Belushi, Bill Murray, Dan Aykroyd, Gilda Radner, etc—in person doing their thing, when the show was at its peak. As we were leaving Rockefeller Center, a group of fans outside started shouting "Jack Cafferty! Jack Cafferty!" Not to be outdone I shouted back at them, "What about me?" Some guy hollered "Who the hell are you?" I shouted back "Jim Zabel, WHO, Des Moines." "Never heard of you," came the answer, "but you must be famous if you're with Jack."

So, start spreading the news, Jack has made it big in New York. He is perfect for the place—the ultimate cynic. I often have people ask me—"Is Cafferty really like that?" I say, "You're seeing him on a good day. You should have worked with him." I say that with affection. Jack was something special. It is one of the top experiences I have had in a career filled with memorable experiences.

The saddest moment in Jack's life occurred a few years ago when he lost his wife Carol. Jack was devoted to her. He was devastated when I talked with him at the time. Later when I called him in New York he said, "It's tough, but I'll make it." Yes, he will. Don't ever bet against this irrepressible Irishman.

Iowa Stadium in Nile Kinnick's day (renamed Kinnick Stadium in 1972)

Nile Kinnick (#24) and his immortal "Iron Men"

With Barb Elliott, Shirley Fry, and Jill Zabel

John Streif (center) "Everybody's Favorite Hawkeye"
with Steve Carfino (left) and Dr. Johnson (right)

Jill and Jim with Ed and Vickie Podolak at the Rose Bowl

With Tom Davis and family (Sherrie and Keno) on the Great Wall

Making a point on "Call Jim Zabel"

KINNICK STADIUM MEDIA WALL OF FAME

Honoring the men who covered Iowa football

Half-time presentation on field for Wall of Fame at Kinnick Stadium, October 28, 2006

In Alba, Iowa honoring Red Frye, the last surviving Iron Man

Jim and Jill visit the Roy Karo Hall of Fame at the University of Iowa, Iowa City

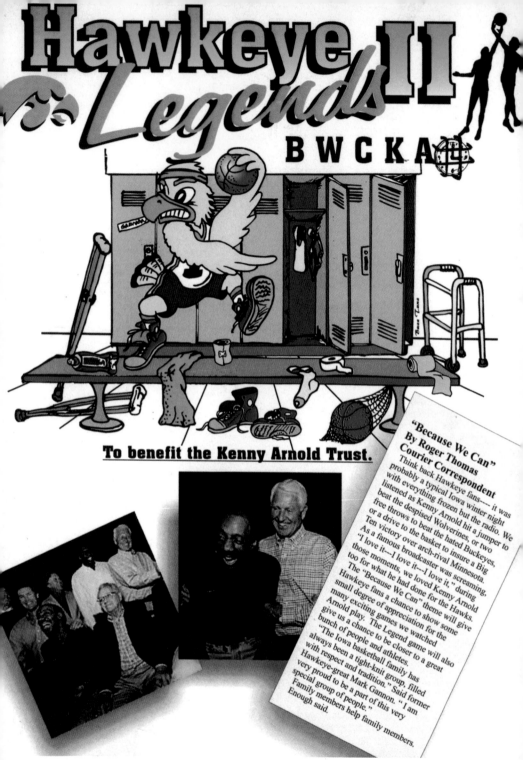

Hawkeye II Legends

BWCKA

To benefit the Kenny Arnold Trust.

"Because We Can"
By Roger Thomas
Courier Correspondent

Think back Hawkeye fans~~~ it was probably a typical Iowa winter night with everything frozen but the radio. We listened as Kenny Arnold hit a jumper to beat the despised Wolverines, or two free throws to beat the hated Buckeyes, or a drive to the basket to insure a Big Ten victory over arch-rival Minnesota. As a famous broadcaster was screaming, "I love it~~I love it~~I love it," during those moments, we loved Kenny Arnold too for what he had done for the Hawks. The "Because We Can" theme will give Hawkeye fans a chance to show some small degree of appreciation for the many exciting games we watched Arnold play. The Legend game will also give us a chance to be closer to a great bunch of people and athletes. "The Iowa basketball family has always been a tight-knit group, filled with respect and tradition." Said former Hawkeye-great Mark Gannon. " I am very proud to be a part of this very special group of people." Family members help family members. Enough said.

1989 team honoring Kenny Arnold

A crazy night on "Beat the Bear" with The Bear and Zabel in his Fruit of the Loom outfit

"Van's Leisure Suit" get-together: Bob Quinn, Jim Zabel, Jerry Reno, Gary Amble

Interviewing Eva Gabor

With Governor Bob and Billie Ray

"World's Largest Tropy" for
"Man of the Year" honor by the
southeast Iowa I-Club (Ottumwa)
presented by president Kendig Kneen

The 40 at 1040 Roast

Clockwise from top left:
Jim and Lute Olson; Emcee Tom Dreesen
with Jill and Jim; Dorothy, Ed, and Joe
Podolak; Emcee Tom Dreesen gets a
laugh from Jim; Joan and Gary Kirke

Clockwise from top left:
Bobby Hansen; Alex Karras and Randy
Duncan; Babe gets a laugh;
Jill and Jim; Jim, Lute Olson, Mary and
Bobby Hansen

Clockwise from top left: Jim and Jill at the head table with Governor Terry Branstad; with Al Couppee; with Twins and Packers TV announcer Ray Scott; Hosts and Guests of Honor: Mr. and Mrs. Gary Kirke with Jim and Jill; Murray Wier, Randy Duncan and Alex Karras

Clockwise from top left:
with WHO benefactors and former
WHO executives Chuck Jewel and
Steve Shannon; Jill and Jim with
Hayden Fry; Sharm Scheuerman,
Hayden Fry, Jim Zabel and Ed
Podolak; Mr. and Mrs. John Ruan III
with host Bill Krause; Bill Krause
and Gary Kirke (with Hayden Fry in
the background)

Enjoying the winter in Scottsdale

Zabel's 75th Roast

Join us for an entertaining evening
of humorous reflection on Jim's 75 years
of life, laughter and the Hawkeyes.

Tuesday, September 3, 1996
Glen Oaks Country Club
Cocktails 6:00 pm   Buffet Dinner 7:00 pm

Proceeds from this event will go to
The Jim Zabel Journalism Scholarship Foundation

RSVP with your check made out to
Jim Zabel Journalism Scholarship Foundation,
by August 28, for $75.00 per person to:
Nancy Cook
c/o Kirke-Van Orsdel
1776 West Lakes Parkway
West Des Moines, IA 50398

Hosted by Gary Kirke and Bill Krause

Spouses/Guests   Sport Coat
Welcome   Casual

Center left: Gary and Curtis with "The Bear"
Center right: Chowing down on a 64 oz. ribeye gave me the nerve to pop the question
Bottom left: Blowing out candles
Bottom right: Proposal Time! Jill laughs: "You can't be serious?" But I was!

Wedding night at the mountain home of Wayne and Carol Carpenter in Scottsdale

Ring Ceremony at the Zabel wedding:
Ed Podolak (Super Bowl),
Jim Zabel (Honorary Iowa Letterman),
Bert Campaneris (World Series),
Bobby Hansen (NBA Championship)

One of my hobbies—raising tomatoes. At one time the Iowa State Fair had a
Jim Zabel Jumbo Tomato Contest.

STAND BY!
"MR. BOLSTER, I'M READY
FOR MY CLOSE-UP"

Bill Bolster is the most rabid Hawkeye fan I know of. He created the Iowa Television Network, which put Lute Olson in our living rooms and touched off a state-wide frenzy for Iowa basketball a few decades ago. One holiday season, he had Forest Evashevski, Randy Duncan and me come to his home in Waterloo to tape a one-hour TV bowl game show. On another occasion, I saw him climb atop a table at a restaurant in Ann Arbor to lead cheers for the Hawkeyes, who were playing Michigan the next day. His rafter-rattling battle cry was "Blue Sucks!!" Bolster left Iowa to manage the NBC television station in St. Louis, which at the time was mired in fourth place in the ratings. Within six months, he had the station in first place. Along the way, he acquired the television rights to St. Louis Cardinals baseball.

The year was 1987. I had just broadcast the Iowa-Ohio State football game which ended with that classic Chuck Hartlieb to Marv Cook pass and a 29-27 Hawkeye victory. The following Monday I got a call from Bolster. He told me he was meeting with his sales staff and he wanted me to replay my final call of the game, so that all of his sales people could hear it on the speaker phone. So I put the tape machine next to the phone and let it go full blast—"Six seconds to play—Hartlieb fades back—he hits Marv Cook!—he's at the 10, he's at the 5—it's a touchdown! It's a touchdown! Ed Podolak is hugging and kissing me!—Oh, my God!, etc., etc." Afterward, Bolster said, "Now, that's selling! Go Hawks!"

Bolster was an entrepreneur and a promoter. He one time brought Ray Scott to town from the Minnesota Twins and Green Bay Packers to do Drake basketball on radio.

After Bolster's success in St. Louis, NBC summoned him to New York to help launch their financial network, CNBC, which was an immediate hit. "Hell, I didn't know anything about Wall Street," Bolster said. "But I guess it's all about money, so that's what counts."

Today, Bolster commutes between a home in Naples, Florida, St. Louis, and New York. He also travels overseas on TV business. When I called him on his cell phone the week of the Ohio State game, he said, "I'm in Italy. I'm going to Venice tomorrow. Maybe I can find a bar that carries the Hawkeyes."

Bill Bolster—one of a kind. The ultimate Hawkeye.

A NIGHT WITH DON HO
"TINY BUBBLES" AND MORE

One of the regular features of my I-Club appearances was to sing the "Hawaiian War Chant". I would say I learned it from Don Ho when I spent a night at the Ho House.

We were going to Honolulu to play Hawaii in football, and Hayden Fry said to me, "You always use that joke about Don Ho, you ought to see him when we're over there. Give him my name, I knew him in the Marine Corps."

So, my wife and I went to the Don Ho show at the Hilton Hawaiian Village. I sent a note backstage about my friendship with Hayden, and he sent a note back for us to meet him in his dressing room after the show.

We went backstage after the show and met Don Ho and his assistant, an attractive young woman of about 28. We drank champagne and talked about Hayden Fry and Iowa football. He said, "the doctors won't let me take a drink. I've had a few in my time. I think I put Chivas Regal out of business."

He then invited us to dinner with him, with one condition, "I know you're media, so no media questions." I agreed. (After all, he was paying.) We had a delightful dinner, and Don Ho regaled us with his stories. He and Elvis were buddies, and they palled around together when Elvis made films in Hawaii. He also was a good friend of Frank Sinatra. "Frank would come to the show a couple times a week when he was making 'From Here to Eternity.'" Then there was Jackie Onassis. "Believe it or not, I pushed her into the pool one night."

He told us the story of how he recorded his all-time hit, "Tiny Bubbles". He said, "I had an all night D.J. show. I was dead-tired at 6 in the morning when my agent came to me with this song he wanted me to record. So we did it, and you know the rest. I've been living off the royalties ever since."

After a few more stories, I asked him, "Where do you live?". He said "That's a media question, I can't answer it." I did get him to agree that he would come on as a halftime guest when I came back to Honolulu in about month to broadcast the Chaminade Classic basketball tournament.

Ed Podolak had a Hawaiian friend named Cal Lui, and I told him about my night with Don Ho. I asked him why Ho wouldn't tell me where he lives. Cal said, "He's got a six million dollar mansion on Diamond Head, and he lives with his three ex-wives and his current girlfriend."

Then I told him that Ho had agreed to come on with me at half-time of the Iowa game in the Chaminade Classic, which would start at noon. Cal Lui laughed, "He doesn't get up until 4 p.m. Good luck!"

Four weeks later, I was broadcasting the Iowa–Eastern Illinois game in Honolulu, when all of a sudden I looked around and saw this guy with big horn rimmed glasses shuffling my way. It was Don Ho! He kept his word, and I kept mine. I didn't ask him anything personal.

SID'S SONG:
"MR. HARTMAN, HATS OFF TO THEE"

Sid Hartman has been the face of the media in Minneapolis for 70 years. He has covered the Gophers, the Vikings, the Twins and a myriad of other sports teams in his newspaper columns and on his radio shows. During that time he has made both friends and enemies among the Iowa media and fans.

He was always competitive and sometimes combative. I remember the time that *Cedar Rapids Gazette* sports editor Gus Schrader and Sid got into a shouting match following an Iowa-Minnesota football game in Minneapolis, after Sid had accused Gus of stealing some stuff from his column in *The Minneapolis Tribune*. They almost came to blows and didn't speak for years afterword.

Sid knew a lot of prominent sports figures, such as Bobby Knight, and he liked to flaunt that fact with a bit of braggadocio—"A close personal friend," is what he loved to say whenever a person of fame was under discussion.

Years ago, at the 1958 Rose Bowl there was a group of us sitting around a table in the Huntington Sheraton Hotel in Pasadena. Sid was there, along with Maury White of the *Des Moines Register*, yours truly and a couple of Chicago sportswriters. Sid started talking in some detail about Iowa's Wing-T Formation and referred to Coach Forest Evashevski as "A close personal friend." I could see that Maury, a former football player himself, (and now the Iowa beat writer) , was doing a slow burn. Sid said, "Evy always calls me to pick him up at the airport." That did it. "Sid," Maury said with a touch of anger in his voice, "why don't you just shut up. You don't know a damn thing about football!" One of the other sportswriters at the table said, "Maury, take it easy." Maury snapped back, "And you know even less!"

When Lou Holtz was coaching at Notre Dame, and Barry Alvarez was his assistant, the Irish played in the Fiesta Bowl. I was covering the game and so was Sid Hartman. He knew Holtz from his days at Minnesota, and he let me know many times that he was "a close personal friend." My buddy, of course, was Barry Alvarez, whom I had known since his days at Iowa, and before that as a state champion high school coach at Mason City.

I had press passes for the game, but Barry gave me one marked "SPECIAL," which was for the press conference after the game.

Notre Dame won. We headed back to the hotel headquarters where the post game press conference with Holtz was going to be held.

I presented my pass marked "SPECIAL." The security guard told me to follow him. He took us into a private room where Holtz and his coaches, including Barry, were relaxing before coming out for the formal press conference.

I taped my interview with Holtz. After that, we all marched out. There was Sid, waiting with his recorder. He saw me and immediately realized I had received preferential treatment. He was irate. "How the hell did you get in here?" he demanded. I answered with great relish, "a close personal friend." Barry got a kick out of that one. Sid didn't.

Barry later said, "Sid might not win a popularity contest, but I'll guarantee you every coach would love to have a guy like him as their beat writer."

Chapter 7

DRAKE & IOWA STATE

Cyclones Steal My Stuff!

BULLDOG TALES

Maury John was a sensible, realistic man, not given to exaggeration. That's why I was astounded by his comments as we were having dinner in Louisville following a disastrous 42-point loss to the Louisville Cardinal basketball team in 1971. (The Bulldogs were called for 33 fouls).

The Drake coach calmly predicted the Bulldogs would win the Missouri Valley Conference race, despite the fact that they were three games behind conference leader Louisville with four games to play.

That's the last time I questioned Maury John's judgment. Drake won its next three games, Louisville lost three, the teams finished in a tie and Drake beat the Cardinals by 15 points in a playoff game at Wichita.

The Bulldogs went on to beat Notre Dame 79-72 in the first round of the NCAA Tournament, then lost to powerhouse Kansas 73-71, ending a brilliant comeback season.

Two years earlier, the Bulldogs reached their all-time peak when they made it to the Final Four, and played perennial champion UCLA a never-to-be-forgotten game. I know I will never forget it because I attended my father's funeral in Aurora, Illinois, then went to O'Hare Airport and flew to Louisville in time for the tip-off at Freedom Hall.

The Bulldog team of Dolph Pulliam, Willie Wise, Willie McCarter and company gave UCLA a classic battle with their renowned "Belly Button" defense, before losing 85-82. Even UCLA coach John Wooden said Drake deserved to win the game.

The Bulldogs walloped North Carolina in the consolation game, 104-84. Maury John left us much too early. He passed away at age 55, but his legacy lives on in Bulldog lore.

P.S. The coach of that Louisville team that beat Drake by 42 points was Howard Stacey, who was soon to become coach at Drake. Actually Stacey was an assistant who was filling in for head coach John Dromo who had fallen ill. When Maury John left Drake for Iowa State after the 1971 season, Athletic Director Bob Karnes reportedly said he was going to hire the coach who gave John his worst beating, and that was Stacey.

Johnny Bright may have been the greatest player ever to don a football uniform in the state of Iowa. He led the nation in total offense for three straight years back in the 1950s, but his most lasting fame came from the lens of an enterprising *Des Moines Register* photographer named Don Ultang. Drake was playing Oklahoma A & M in Stillwater, where black players were not too welcome in those days. On a play where Bright  was completely out of the action, an Oklahoma A & M player ran up and slugged him with his elbow, breaking his jaw. Ultang caught the whole thing on his machine-gun camera, which showed the incident frame-by-frame in sequence. He flew back to Des Moines and it made headlines in the *Register* the next day. The paper and Ultang won a Pulitzer Prize. After Oklahoma A & M refused to apologize for the incident, Drake dropped out of the Missouri Valley Conference. That same weekend, Iowa and beleaguered Coach Leonard Raffensperger lost to Michigan 21-0, but this was completely overshadowed by the Bright incident. Sportscaster Al Couppee, no fan of the Hawkeye coach, told the Des Moines press club at our Monday meeting—"Bright's jaw saved Raffensperger's ass."

The injury ended Bright's collegiate career, but he became a super-star in Canada, earning All-Pro honors nine straight years.

I vividly remember "Johnny Bright Night" at Drake Stadium. *Des Moines Register & Tribune* sportswriter Maury White, a former Drake football star himself, helped to emcee the occasion along with yours truly. Maury gave me a wink when he got up and said "I'm here because of a misunderstanding, someone told me it was Maury White Night." After that, he launched into praise of Bright, and I followed with more of the same. Bright obliged by going out the next day and scoring four touchdowns against a reputable Detroit team. Bright spent most of his off-seasons in Des Moines. He was a teacher and an outstanding softball pitcher.

I was a great friend of Johnny and did many interviews with him through the years. I delivered one of the eulogies at his funeral. He passed away in 1983 at the age of 53. He died on the operating table of a heart attack while undergoing knee surgery. During his collegiate career, Johnny Bright set an NCAA total offense record of 5,983 yards.

I have had a 70-year love affair with the Drake Relays. I ran in them when I was in high school and I have covered them as a broadcaster ever since. I first ran at Drake for Davenport High School in 1938 and again in 1939 when I captained the Blue Devil Track Team. We won the mile relay and Ronald Reagan, just back from Hollywood, presented us with our medals. (I interviewed him for our school newspaper, *The Blackhawk*.)

Only the venerable Paul Morrison outranks me in Relays attendance, and I have as much chance of catching him as I did Jesse Owens when I once ran against the Olympic star. Anyway, when you ask about the Relays it all comes down to

Left: 1950 Drake Relays: Interviewing the nation's #1 miler of that era, Don Gehrmann

Below: Paul Morrison, "Mr. Drake"

With Iowa coach Dick Schultz and Drake coach Maury John

With my all-time hero, Jesse Owens on WHO-TV

greatest performers and performances. I have spent hours talking and debating these very things with Paul, the late Jim Duncan and others.

Invariably, the four record breaking performances in the mile run by Jim Ryun (1966), Steve Scott (1979), Alan Webb (2004) and Bernard Lagat (2007) should rank near the top of the list. After that, it's a grab-bag of personal choices. I covered that epic 100-meter race between Bobby Morrow and Dave Sime in 1956 for NBC, so that is also high on my list.

For a long time I favored 1951, when Drake swept the three sprint relays, 440, 880 and mile (before metric distances). A number of high school memories linger with me. Clyde Duncan, Jim Kirby, Ceasar Smith, and those great Valley mile relay teams rank high.

The North High "Flying Four" of 1948 (Gary Scott, George Nichols, Connie Jones and Reggie Kaiser) had a faster qualifying time in the 880-yard relay than the University of Texas. (I ran against Reggie Kaiser's older brother Frank, of Des Moines East, when I was in high school, and I saw a lot of his back). There is another moment that stays with me because of the performer—Tim Dwight. I was talking to Tim on the infield at the Boys' State high school track meet at Drake. He had already won the 100 and 200. He heard an announcement and said he had to leave. He explained that teammate Joey Woody had been injured in an auto accident and he was going to fill in for him in the 400-meter hurdles. "How many times have you run them?" I asked. "Never," he said. With that he left for the starting blocks. Guess who won? You know who did. Tim Dwight.

CYCLONE CONNECTION

Gary Thompson is generally considered the ultimate Iowa State Cyclone. I believe most sports fans probably would put me in the same position with the Iowa Hawkeyes. That being the case, it's interesting, I think, how much and how often our two lives have intersected. Gary is one of my best friends. When I was under the weather with pneumonia and other ills in the winter of 2009, Gary called me three times.

Our relationship began when he was a 16-year-old basketball star at Roland High School, and I was starting my play-by-play sports career at WHO. We were doing a high school game of the week and one of the first schools we selected was Roland. We did the Rockets game with Ogden and later the return game at Ogden. They were both hot teams. Roland also hired me as speaker at their athletic banquet. Gary and I have often laughed about what happened afterward. Basketball Coach Buck Cheadle invited me to his house in Roland and we had a couple of beers. When I left, Cheadle asked me to take the empty beer cans with me. "I don't dare leave them in the trash can here," he said, "You know what people would think." So, I helped to destroy the evidence and the Norwegian community of Roland stayed clean and pure.

Gary Thompson (center) interviewing Digger Phelps

I broadcast all of Gary's and Roland's appearances in the Boys' state tournament, where the Rockets always played well, and in the championship one year. I also broadcast Gary's games at Iowa State, when the Cylcones beat Wilt "The Stilt" Chamberlain at Kansas in a major upset. Gary was the big reason for the Cyclone victory.

Our next get-together came when Gary finished his collegiate and Phillips 66 playing career. At that time we were doing Iowa State and Drake Basketball games in addition to Iowa. Gary was my color man and analyst for Cyclone games, and he was a good one. Everyone in the Big 8 (later Big 12) conference respected him. That was good, because we had some ticklish moments. One of them occurred when Iowa State played Missouri and Coach Norm Stewart, who was known as "Stormin' Norm" for good reason.

Missouri was one of the top-rated teams in the nation, but they had been upset by Kansas State earlier in the week and now Iowa State was getting the best of them. The Cyclones won by two points. Norm was so mad he kicked the water cooler, then stalked into the locker room. The Missouri sports information director announced that Stewart would allow only certain reporters to interview him—Gary was one of the select few. I gave Gary my recorder and asked him to get the interview. When Gary returned, his face was flushed. He said "You better preview that tape before you play it." During a long commercial and score break, I listened to the first part of the tape. Gary asked "Norm, last Saturday you were beaten by Kansas State by two points. Tonight, Iowa State also beat you by two. What happened?"

Norm answered in a bitter tone, "The same thing happened tonight that happened last Saturday. We got f_ _ _ _." Naturally, I rolled the tape past this part and used the rest of it. But I kept the tape. The Iowa State game was on Thursday. Saturday I went to Iowa City to do the Big-10 game between Iowa and Illinois. Before the game, I taped an interview with Illini Coach Lou Henson and his assistant Tony Yates. After the interview I

Above: Gary Thompson, "Mr. Iowa State"

Left: Gary Thompson and "The Mayor," new Iowa State coach Fred Hoiberg

played back the one we had done with Norm Stewart for Henson and Yates, since Illinois and Missouri were also big rivals. Lou and Tony got a big kick out of it. Iowa beat Illinois by two points that night. I sent my color man, Sharm Scheuerman, down to the locker room to do a post game interview with Henson. The Illinois coach said, "Tell Zabel that the same thing that happened to Missouri last week happened to us tonight." That's putting it directly.

In those days the Iowa State football and basketball departments were split by deep divisions caused by one man, Athletic Director Lou McCullough. (A fact well-documented by Chuck Offenburger in his excellent book on Gary Thompson.) I also observed it first hand when I was doing Cyclone basketball. I actually got along with McCullough myself because I was a

Big 10 guy and so was he really, even though he was at a Big 8 school. Lou spent years as assistant football coach at Ohio State, and his fondest wish, which became an obsession with him, was to become head coach of the Buckeyes.

I knew what was happening at Ohio State, and Lou loved to discuss it with me, but it rankled other people. Former player Dan Grimm served as analyst on the Cyclone football broadcasts and he was no guy to mess with. They were interviewing McCullough after a game, and Lou kept referring to his coaching days and telling how "we" did it. Finally Grimm grabbed him and demanded angrily "What 'we' are you talking about? You're not at Ohio State anymore, you're at Iowa State." McCullough never did get back to Ohio State. Two former Cyclones, Earle Bruce and John Cooper, passed him by in the race for head coaching job for the Buckeyes.

Lou stayed at Iowa State and was the center of turmoil to the end. After the death of Maury John, assistant Gus Guydon became acting head coach and was immediately at odds with McCullough. Then McCullough hired and fired two basketball coaches, Ken Trickey and Lynn Nance. And on top of that he tried to get Gary Thompson fired from his network television job on the Big 12 Game of the Week.

I can verify how bad things were when I was doing an Iowa State—Colorado game in Boulder. Lynn Nance invited me to go to dinner with him. I liked Nance. He spoke his mind, and he did not like McCullough. As we walked into the restaurant, there was McCullough with a couple of guys. Nance said, "Let's get as far away as possible," so we went to the other side of the room. Nance was fired soon after that. This led to McCullough's most famous act, the much-publicized hiring of Johnny Orr, who was (and is) one of my all-time favorite people. I got to know him well at Michigan, where he regaled us with unrepeatable Bobby Knight stories, then I did his games at Iowa State and his pre-and post-coaches shows and had him as a premier guest on "Beat the Bear," one of our most popular

With Johnny Orr, a Cyclone pal

TV shows. I also traveled with him. He loved it when we broadcast his games because all of his recruits could hear them around the country. He and Hayden got along famously. I always felt he was Iowa State's best goodwill ambassador.

When Dan McCarney brought Iowa State to the Insight Bowl to play Pittsburgh in 2000, I went to the Cyclones' pep rally at the convention center in Phoenix. A radio guy spotted me. He asked , "How does it feel to be with 8,000 Cyclone fans?" I said, "I feel like a Catholic in Salt Lake City."

Actually, I didn't feel that much out of place. McCarney was one of my best friends from the coaching ranks. I knew him from his playing and coaching days at Iowa. My oldest daughter, Jane, attended Iowa State, as did three grandchildren. I am proud of all of them. As of this writing, my youngest grandson, Charlie Paul, is on the cross country team at Iowa State.

I have told them that my love for my family runs deep, but my colors, Old Gold & Black, are indelible.

Love him or hate him, Zabel is an Iowa legend

"I LOVE IT, I LOVE IT, I LOVE IT!!!"

Anybody who follows Iowa football and basketball on WHO Radio of Des Moines has heard this, and many other trademark lines, from Jim Zabel often in his 43 years of broadcasting Hawkeye athletics.

Love him or hate him, Zabel is as much a part of Hawkeye lore as Hayden Fry and Lute Olson.

Zabel

"The average Hawkeye fan would rather listen to us," said the veteran broadcaster. "There are three stations currently originating broadcasts, but the surveys show we get the majority of the listeners."

After 43 years in the business, the energetic Zabel, who

Mike Condon

Nonpareil Sports Writer

SPEAKING OF SWI

was in Council Bluffs last Thursday as a part of the Nile Kinnick I-Club's yearly gathering, has no immediate retirement plans.

"My standard line is that I went to my doctor . . . and he told me the mouth was the last thing to go," he said with his familiar laugh. "Seriously, I've got an open-end contract with WHO and I hope to be there as long as I'm able."

"YOUR LISTENING TO THE HOME AND AWAY VOICE OF THE IOWA HAWK-EYES."

Some day real soon, WHO may be the only station able to make that claim.

Iowa is one of the few schools that doesn't have an exclusive radio contract. Besides WHO, KHAK and WMT of Cedar Rapids, have carried the Hawkeyes for a number of years and have built their own audiences with such broadcast veterans as Bob Brooks, Ron Gonder and Frosty Mitchell.

Zabel believes Iowa isn't far away from going exclusive.

"I would think in the next five years there will be exclusivity," he said. "Our station has a great chance to get the contract. I think we have the best network. Our anchor station is 50,000 watts clear channel and can be heard coast-to-coast at night.

"This will be our 61st year of doing Iowa athletics as a station," he added. "We've been doing the Hawkeyes longer than anybody."

"GIVE THOSE RADIOS A BIG HUG AND A KISS."

Zabel knows he has a love-hate relationship with Hawkeye fans all over the country.

He makes no bones about the fact he is rooting for Iowa to win.

"My job is to get listeners," says Zabel. "You are never going to get 100 percent of them and you will never satisfy all the ones you have."

The high-strung, emotional style Zabel uses endears him to many; but annoys many others.

"Hawkeye fans listen to us for a reason," he said. "Some listen because they want to hear what Zabel said this time. Most fans are familiar with us; they like us; they all in love with us. We give them that Iowa slant."

"LET'S RECOGNIZE OUR GREAT GROUP OF AFFIL-

IATES."

For listeners in southwest Iowa and eastern Nebraska, finding the Hawkeyes on radio, especially during the day, has been difficult.

For the past two seasons, Iowa football was heard on KKAR-AM (1180 in Omaha). The station did basketball two years ago, but dropped Tom Davis' team in favor of Omaha Lancer hockey.

Zabel knows there is a large number of Iowa fans in this area.

"We're not saying we're bigger than Nebraska in their own back yard," he said. "We know there are an awful lot of Iowa fans over here — many more than people realize."

KJAN-AM (1220 in Atlantic) has been added to the network for next season. Zabel said negotiations are ongoing with KOIL-AM (1290 in Omaha) to carry football, and possibly basketball.

"THE HAWKEYES HAVE WON IT. THE HAWKEYES WIN."

When a broadcaster has done over 6,000 games in a career, biggest thrills are hard to find.

"One of the biggest thrills I get is just walking into the broadcasting booth," says Zabel.

The memories for Zabel are many, but he picked a pair of football games as two of his top thrills.

"When Hayden went to the Rose Bowl in 1981, we beat Michigan up there 9-7 on their Homecoming," he said. "Then there was the game two years ago when we went back up to Michigan and beat them 24-23, again on their Homecoming."

Zabel went on to talk of Iowa's going to the Final Four in basketball in 1980 and Davis' team winning the Maui Classic in his second season.

In other words, it's been quite a ride for the dean of broadcasters in the Big Ten.

■ LIFESTYLES:

Chapter 8

ABOUT STEERS & BEERS

In August, All Roads Lead to the State Fair

"OUR STATE FAIR IS A GREAT STATE FAIR, DON'T MISS IT, DON'T EVEN BE LATE— IT'S DOLLARS TO DONUTS THAT OUR STATE FAIR IS THE BEST STATE FAIR IN THE STATE!"

Rogers and Hammerstein apparently thought so, as their musical attests. So did Hollywood. There were three "State Fair" films, all based on Phil Stong's best-selling novel, written when he was a young *Des Moines Register* reporter in the 1930s. He wrote about the mythical Frakes family and their adventures during a week at the Iowa State Fair. The story reportedly was based on a real family from Columbus Junction, Iowa.

The first "State Fair" movie, in 1933, starred Janet Gaynor and Will Rogers; The second, in 1945, was the Rodgers & Hammerstein musical starring Jeanne Crain, Dick Haymes and Dana Andrews, and the third, in 1962, had Pat Boone and Alice Faye in the title roles. All three starred "Blue Boy," the Grand Champion Boar. (For the record, the original Blue Boy was the brother of "Floyd of Rosedale", the legendary pig of Iowa-Minnesota football fame.)

I had a running contest with two of my late contemporaries, George Mills of the *Des Moines Register*, and Bill Riley, as to who attended the most State Fairs. My record, as of this writing, stands at 58. I don't know whether I will ever pass the other two, even though they are gone, but their legacy will live as long as the fair itself.

Many people deserve credit for the tremendous growth and success of the fair. Two that I would like to single out are Don Greiman and Kenny Falk. Don, a long time personal friend, has served on the State Fair Board of directors for 40 years, as of this writing. Years ago he told me, "As successful as we are, we've got to do one more thing. We've got to get the people from Des Moines and other large cities to come to the fair. We're not just an agricultural and livestock show."

So what has happened? Des Moines real estate mogul Bill Knapp and his wife spend the entire run of the fair on the camp grounds each year, and they donated over one million dollars to heat and cool the Varied Industries Building for year-round use.

Des Moines businessman Gary Kirke owns one of the largest eating establishments on the grounds, and he often throws gratis beer parties in front of the Grandstand. Other Des Moines power brokers, like Bill Krause, are often seen on the grounds.

The late Kenny Falk was a tireless promoter of the fair when he served as Secretary. He made countless trips around the state, along with our dear departed friend, Shie Foudree, promoting the fair. I think the two of them appeared at or worked with every service club in Des Moines.

I have so many memories of the fair I can't count them all— Radio and TV shows, calling the auto races and Demo Derbies, and perilous adventures on the Midway. (My wife, Jill, dared me to go on the "Moonraker." I think part of my body is still there).

When it comes to abject fear, nothing equals the Celebrity Steer Show. I agreed to be in the show along with Iowa Women's basketball Coach Vivian Stringer. She either had a gentle animal, or knew all the right things to say to it—mine was a monster who hated me from the outset. It's one thing to see those huge four legged animals from afar, and another to lead them around the show ring. My steer weighed 1200 pounds! Do you realize what that would be like rolling on top of you?! That's all I could think about as I tried to maneuver the massive beast around the ring.

Finally, it stopped dead, then it snorted and bucked. The 11-year-old kid who raised the animal appeared on the scene, carrying a long prod. He shouted, "Stop that!" and gave the steer a sharp whack across the hind quarters. The animal trembled like a leaf. Then the kid put his prod underneath the steer. "He likes to be rubbed down there," the kid said. (Who doesn't?) He suddenly grew passive, and brought the second highest price during the auction that followed.

*Testing my bravery
at the Celebrity Steer
Show, Iowa State Fair*

I often wondered what those steaks were like.

I was doing a one hour noon-time show from the Iowa State Fair on WHO-TV. After 10 days, we were getting to the bottom of the barrel on interview guests. Bob Scarpino, an enterprising young director who was working with me, said he had seen a guy walking the grounds who claimed that he was Abraham Lincoln. "Sounds great," I said. "Let's get him."

So, Honest Abe appeared and he indeed looked the part. There was the stovepipe hat, the beard, the swallowtail coat and the long, lanky frame. I asked him how he could prove to us he was Lincoln. He recited the Gettysburg Address verbatim. Then he talked about his generals, the war, his wife Mary and family.

He almost had me convinced. I thanked him. He turned and walked away. Squarely in the middle of his back was a large sign that read "Eat at Curt Yocum's."

Curt had one of the largest lunch counters at the fair, and a big restaurant in Iowa City. He was a red-hot Iowa fan, and his son, Brandt was a starter for the Hawkeyes.

A wonderful era: girls 6-on-6 basketball— We loved it!

Incidentally, my State Fair TV director, Bob Scarpino, also directed telecasts of the Girls' state tournament and was responsible for those spectacular halftime shows. They were exciting and colorful always. There simply has never been anything like six-player girls basketball.

I love it and I loved the girls who played it—Denise Long, Jeanette Olson, Peg Peterson, Janet Mostaert, Sandy VanCleave, Joyce Elder, Deb Coates, Lynn Lorenzen, to mention a few. If E. Wayne Cooley is the P.T. Barnum of girls basketball, Bob Scarpino is the Busby Berkeley (and if you don't know who Busby Berkeley is, check out Turner Classic Movies).

No State Fair report would be complete without mentioning the tremendous job that WHO's Van and Bonnie do in promoting this great event. Who else could draw 20,000 people, waiting for the Fair Gates to open at 5:30 a.m.? Van says it's the free corn dogs that do the trick, but I say it's the power of their top-rated show. They also draw record numbers of accordion players, chocolate lovers and supporters to save the Battleship Iowa from salvage.

It's always a thrill to be on their show. I did it when we were all in Hawaii for a Hawkeye football game. Because of the five-hour time differential I was coming in just as they were going on. It was perfect! And they didn't even have to give me a corn dog!

I can't say enough about my partner on "Sound Off," Jon Miller. He once told me that as a kid growing up in West Branch, he used to hide in the closet and pretend he was Jim Zabel broadcasting a game. Today when I work with him, I say "Jon is the "knowledge" and I am the "history." He also does a Thursday night round-table show on the Big 10 TV network which has been one of the major media success stories in the nation the last couple of years. I predict big things for Jon. His growth coincides with the dramatic expansion of the Big 10 Conference. I can't help but remember what Nebraska's Bob Devaney told me in an interview years ago. He said, "I'd give my eyeteeth to belong to the Big 10". Now belatedly, he gets his wish and the Hawkeyes get another, and possibly bigger, natural rivalry.

ZABEL FAN CLUB THRIVING IN IOWA CITY

TURNBULL

ZABEL FANS — You may be interested to know that the Jim Zabel Fan Club is alive, well and growing — and that's no joke.

The WHO radio-TV sports director regularly broadcasts all University of Iowa football and basketball games, and last year a group of Hawkeye students formed a fan club for him.

They're going to hold a second annual dinner in his honor at the Quadrangle dormitory in Iowa City tonight before the Iowa-Indiana game.

"Last year I thought it was a joke when they had the first dinner," Zabel said. "I expected about 12 guys to show up and there were 350 people there. Now they tell me they've got 2,000 in the fan club."

When Carl Wiederanders of Dubuque, the club's president, wrote to Zabel and asked him to pick a suitable date for this year's gathering, he concluded the letter by saying: "We are anxiously awaiting word from the greatest WHO personality, not Ronald Reagan but Jim Zabel."

Zabel says he is so thrilled by this outpouring of affection that he may even pick up the check tonight.

The Fan Club had 2,000 members at one time!

Chapter 9

ZABEL-PALOOZA

There's No Expiration Date on Fun

A ROAST TO TOAST

Gary Kirke is known as a guy who gets things done. And in a big way. That is why, when he announced he was planning a roast for me in 1989, I knew it would be something spectacular. He never does anything half-way, or even seven-eighths, for that matter. I was prepared to be overwhelmed, and I was. But, honestly, I really didn't expect the invitations to be in the form of a tape recorded message from President Ronald Reagan, all neatly packaged in a shiny black box with lettering reading "President Ronald Reagan invites you to Toast Jim Zabel."

The theme of the roast was "40 at 1040", reflecting the number of years I had broadcast Iowa Football on WHO (1949-1989), at that time.

Everything was "A-Number-One-Top-Of-The-Heap," to paraphrase Frank Sinatra. In fact, Gary flew Sinatra's lead-in man, Tom Dreesen, in from Las Vegas, to serve as emcee.

Dreesen established his line of fire with this: "I don't tell ethnic jokes because my mother is Italian and my father is Irish. Not every Italian is a member of the Mafia, and not every Irishman is a drunk. However, Puerto Ricans do steal hubcaps!!"

Of course he had to tell a Sinatra story. Frank asks Dean Martin, "Is it true you joined Alcoholics Anonymous?" Martin said it was. Frank asks "Did you stop drinking?" Martin says, "No, but I changed my name."

President Ronald Reagan invites you to toast Jim Zabel

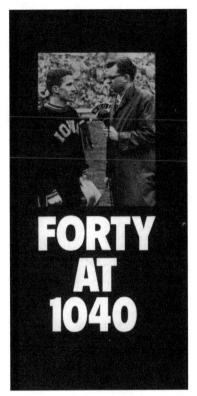

Next, he took off on me and my "Let's Go Bowling Show". He said, "Zabel was practically raised in a bowling alley. But then tragedy struck. His whole family lost their jobs when automatic pin setters came in."

So that's how the evening went. The list of roasters read like a celebrity all-star roster for that time—Tom Brokaw, Evy, Hayden, Lute, Tom Davis, Alex Karras, Sens. Harkin and Grassley, Gov. Branstad, to name a few, and of course my buddy, Ed Podolak, who said, "When I was a kid, I listened to Jim Zabel on this radio, in my folk's kitchen."

He produced the little ivory colored Zenith radio. "Jim Zabel was my favorite sportscaster. Of course, the only station we could get was WHO."

A banner evening! A black-tie affair in the Grand Ballroom of the Des Moines Marriott. At $250 a plate, it enabled us to establish two "Jim Zabel Scholarships" at the University of Iowa Journalism School.

So thanks to everyone who helped to make it such a memorable event. Scott Smith for his marvelous music, Bev Davis for the great decorations, the late Al Barcheski for the videos, and members of the planning committee, especially Bill Krause, and a host of others.

But most of all, thanks to Gary Kirke—A guy who gets things done! (One person he really impressed was my wife-to-be, Jill, who sat at the head table with me).

Jim Zabel
Immortalization
and
Roast

The Committee
to Immortalize and Roast Jim Zabel
welcomes you to an evening of entertainment
for a good cause.
Contributions will be tax deductible.
The proceeds from this event will be donated
to the Jim Zabel Scholarship Fund
at the University of Iowa Foundation.

Roast Agenda

6:00 PM   COCKTAILS

7:00 PM   DINNER

8:00 PM   ROAST

Program

Master of Ceremonies
TOM DREESEN

Honorary Roast Chairman
GOVERNOR TERRY BRANSTAD

Invocation
SISTER PATRICIA CLARE SULLIVAN

Roasters
TOM BROKAW – VIDEO
ED PODOLAK
AL COUPPEE
FOREST EVASHEVSKI – VIDEO
RANDY DUNCAN
BILL REICHARDT
DR. BRECHLER (ACKNOWLEDGMENT)
GOVERNOR ROBERT RAY – VIDEO
BOBBY COMMINGS
SHARM SCHEUERMAN
SENATOR HARKIN – VIDEO
CARL CAIN
RAY SCOTT
MURRAY WIER
WAYNE COOLEY (ACKNOWLEDGMENT)
BABE BISIGNANO
BUMP ELLIOTT
COACH TOM DAVIS
COACH HAYDEN FRY
HUNTER RAWLINGS
HEIDI SOLIDAY
CHUCK LONG
JOHN JOHNSON
SENATOR GRASSLEY – VIDEO
BUCK TURNBULL
MAURY WHITE
JULIE GAMMACK
JON LAZAR
STEVE KRAFCISIN
DAN POMEROY
BOBBY HANSEN
LUTE OLSON
ALEX KARRAS

Jim Zabel Remarks

Video Presentation

Committee Chairman
BILL KRAUSE

SIGNATURE LINES

The standard greeting I usually get from friends these days is not "Hello, how are you?" But rather, "I Love It, I Love It, I Love It." That seems to have become my identifying catchphrase. I guess it's flattering since they had to be listening to pick up that tag line. It has become the No. 1 question I get all the time—how did it start?

First, let me explain. If you were to question 100 sportscasters about their signature lines, the great majority would tell you, "it just happened—it wasn't planned or premeditated." That's the way it was with me. It took place on January 22, 1987, at Carver Hawkeye Arena. Tom Davis' Hawkeyes became the first team to score more than 100 points on a Bob Knight Indiana team. (101-87 was the final). Isn't that reason enough to exult? I think so. Being an emotional broadcaster anyway, it just came out of my mouth almost automatically—"I Love It! I Love It! I Love It!" I repeated it a couple more times and I felt then, as I do now, that it expressed the inner feelings of most Hawkeye fans. So, keep it up. I Love It!

As far as my other signature line is concerned, "Hug and kiss your radios," I'm almost embarrassed to explain the story behind it. But here goes. A woman had sent me a picture of her cat on top of her radio, and she said "I named my cat Jim Zabel because every time you come on the air with a game, the cat jumps on top of the radio and starts to purr."

The next game Iowa played went right down to the wire and was decided by a Hawkeye player at the free throw line. Suddenly, as I was describing the action, the image of that cat raced into my mind. Almost subconsciously I said "hug and kiss your radios." The phrase stuck. I added, "but not while you're driving." Crazy, isn't it? Incidentally, the guy made the free throws and Iowa won the game. So thanks to Jim Zabel, the cat.

QUOTES OF NOTE

Iowa basketball stars Eddie Horton and Roy Marble were known as two guys you didn't mess with. One night they got into a fight in downtown Iowa City during which they decked a couple of Hawkeye wrestlers. Iowa finished second in the NCAA wrestling championships that year. Coach Dan Gable told the wrestling banquet crowd, "We would have finished first if we'd had Horton and Marble."

Dan Gable at work

◇◇◇

Mark Harmon is the son of Michigan great Tom Harmon, and he played football at UCLA before turning to acting. I happened to mention to Evashevski what a good-looking guy young Harmon was. "Yeah," Evy said, "I'd like to reel him out in hotel lobbies."

◇◇◇

My late friend Bill Reichardt was sometimes controversial and always colorful. He liked to say that Tim Dwight was the second-best football player to come out of City High School in Iowa City. Of course, Reichardt himself played for City High. My favorite story about his high school exploits is one relayed to me by Bud Legg of the State Association, which inducted Reichardt into its hall of fame in 2009. Reichardt was in the locker room after a game in which he scored four touchdowns. He asked a teammate, "Does All-State have a hyphen in it?" The teammate said he didn't know. In the next game, a week later, Reichardt fumbled three times and did not score a point. After the game, his teammate told him, "I know that "Honorable Mention" does not have a hyphen in it." After his days at

City High, Reichardt went to the University of Iowa, where he became the Hawkeyes leading ground-gainer. He was named MVP of the Big 10 in 1951. More than that, he became the first player in history to earn MVP from a team that did not win a Big 10 game. I can remember interviewing him at halftime of a Hawkeye basketball game after he had received his trophy. He said, "Not bad for a guy who did not play in a winning Big 10 game. At least I made *Ripley's Believe It or Not.*"

During one of his many Rose Bowl telecasts, Dick Enberg revealed that John Phillip Sousa considered Michigan's fight song, "The Victors," to be one of the three greatest marches ever written. I interviewed Dick on my show later that year and asked him, "What were the other two marches that Sousa liked?" Without hesitation he said, "Washington Post and Stars and Stripes Forever." That's called doing your homework. Incidentally, Enberg paid tribute to all of us radio play-by-play guys when he said, "You're lucky. You're still doing the games on radio." I said, "But all of us would give our eyeteeth to have your job on TV." He said, "Yeah, it's great. But I still think of my old radio days. On TV, the picture tells the story. On radio, you're it—you're the whole show." You know? He was right. I've done both. Radio is a lot more fun. Our battle cry before the games was "Turn up the sound!" and an amazing number of people did. In fact, one of our key radio sponsors asked me if he was buying TV time because so many people turned up the radio broadcast to cover the TV audio.

Michigan vs. Ohio State has been called the greatest rivalry in all of sports. How deep do the feelings go? I'll tell you, because I saw them first-hand. Following an Iowa-Michigan game in Iowa City, I was interviewing the Wolverines' legendary broadcaster, Bob Ufer. He's the man whose pronunciation of "Meeshigan", as Fielding Yost used to call it, made him famous. While I was doing the interview, my producer leaned over and whispered to me, "The Ohio State guy is standing outside. He won't come in." The "guy" was Esco Sarkkinen, Woody Hayes' number one assistant, who was scouting Iowa. After finishing the Ufer interview, we went to a break and I had to go down the hallway to retrieve Sarkkinen. "Why didn't you come in?" I asked him. He said, "You've heard of oil and water? I'm talking about maize and blue and scarlet and gray. They don't mix either."

My favorite Hawkeye trivia question: The greatest Iowa basketball player of all time never wore a varsity uniform, who was he? Give up? The answer: Connie Hawkins. He was the most amazing player of his day. A 6-foot 8-inch point guard, he could dribble two basketballs the length of the court and dunk them both. I saw him do it when he played on the Iowa freshman team (before freshmen were eligible for varsity play). Hawkins was recruited by Coach Sharm Scheuerman, but was in trouble from the start, both in and out of school. He was blacklisted by the NBA for his alleged association with gamblers and other charges (which were never proven). He played a number of years with the Harlem Globetrotters. His name was eventually cleared, and he went on to become a superstar in the old ABA. After that, he spent the rest of his career in the NBA and became so outstanding that even the legendary Dr. J came to him for advice about his game. He was an All-Star for years.

I ran into Connie when he worked in public relations for the Phoenix Suns. Connie called me "Mr. Hawkeye." I told him, "You were Magic Johnson before Magic Johnson." Connie said, "Hey, I think I like that," and he had me tell the Suns' broadcaster Al McCoy, a longtime buddy since our WHO days together. Al said, "Connie was Magic and Dr. J combined. He could start on any team in the country." I added, "Even Iowa."

Now, a quote that I am very proud of from a book by Dick Vitale: "When I am driving down the highway on a winter night, the three voices I want to hear are Woody Durham doing North Carolina basketball, Caywood Ledford doing Kentucky, or Jim Zabel doing Iowa. They are the best."

Bobby Knight and controversy have always gone hand-in-hand. A few years ago, sportswriter John Feinstein did a book on Indiana basketball called *Season on the Brink*. The unique aspect of the writing arrangement was that Knight gave Feinstein total access to his locker room, practices, travel accommodations—even his home. He also gave Feinstein permission to quote him verbatim, blue language and all. After the book came out, with much fanfare, Knight decided he didn't like it. The language was too raw, even for him. About this time, I interviewed Feinstein at half-time of the Iowa-Purdue game in West Lafayette. I asked him, "How are you getting along with Knight?" He said, "Terrible. He hates me. Last week he called me a whore. This week he said I was a pimp. I wish he would make up his mind so I know how to dress."

George Raveling liked to talk about his tough childhood in Washington D.C. He told me, "One day I asked a guy how far it was to the subway. He said, 'I don't know. Nobody's ever made it.'" George said, "If you saw a guy with two ears, it meant he was new to the area." His high school, he said, had the "only school newspaper in the country with an obituary column." I still treasure a gift that I received from George—three bottles of wine, with labels that read, "Jim Zabel and George Raveling—A Love Affair". (Now, don't jump to conclusions. We are both happily married men. George was a very emotional guy.) He also had a great sense of humor. One time on a team flight to Columbus, Ohio, George announced on the P.A. system, "I've got good news and bad news from the pilot. The bad news is we're lost. The good news is we're really making good time."

Jim Zabel, well known sportscaster from WHO radio and television in Des Moines, took time last week to visit the site of the movie, "Field of Dreams." Zabel said he attended the movie premiere in Dubuque and wanted to visit the baseball field. He said he was impressed with the condition of the field and was surprised at the large number of people who were at the field on a Friday afternoon. He said he would like to attend the Upper Deck Field of Dreams fantasy game on Labor Day if he can arrange his schedule.

Chapter 10

FINAL THOUGHTS

Diane at the lake

Memories to Cherish

ALL IN THE FAMILY

One day when my youngest daughter, Diane, was about eighteen months old, I took her to the park across the street from our Beaverdale home. Some kindergarten kids from Byron Rice School walked by, and one of them asked, "Is it going to be a boy or a girl?"

Register columnist Donald Kaul lived up the street from us, and we used to alternate taking our kids to nursery school in the wintertime. Don and I both agreed there was nothing quite like bundling up three kids in snowsuits and boots on a cold winter morning and making sure they all got safely in the car. In fact, I think Don did a very amusing column on kids and snowsuits. (He also did some very good ones on girls basketball and Des Moines' tar-and-gravel streets in the hot summertime.)

Despite a hectic work schedule, I was able to spend a lot of time with my kids when they were little. One reason was that I did all the driving in our family. My wife and I had been in a serious auto accident shortly after we were married, and she

Yes, I did mow my own lawn!

I loved to water ski when I was younger. Friend Sam Zoeckler had the boat.

never drove again after that. I did all the grocery shopping, and would usually take the kids with me. They loved "going to the store". Then there were dancing lessons, gymnastics, Sunday School and trips to the doctor.

My married life started in February of 1946, when I took a girl from Odgen, Iowa to the altar. Her name was Mary Janice Boehm. We met when I was covering the Drake Relays and she was in the Queen's Court. A Kappa sorority sister introduced us.

Our first child, Jane, came along in 1952. Diane was born eight years later. Because of the age differential, I spent fourteen consecutive years going to "Parents' Night" at Bryon Rice. Someone once said, "Don't marry a sportscaster. The last time you'll see him will be on your wedding day, and then he'll probably have to leave early to go to a game."

There is some truth to that. There are no plateaus in the radio-television business. You are either successful, and sponsors all want you to do their shows, or you are not a hot commodity, and you may wish you had become a plumber.

In my case, I was already working a seven-day week, including most holidays, with a full play-by-play schedule of football and basketball, plus assorted specialty shows, like "Let's Go

Bowling" and "Beat the Bear" on WHO-TV, and "Call Jim Zabel" on WHO Radio. Obviously, you have to love what you do—and I did. Plus, the income is welcome and necessary.

The kids really looked forward to summer vacations. For eighteen straight years, we spent two to three weeks at Lake Okoboji each summer. I loved the lake. We all had a lot of friends there.

My job had its perks that benefitted my family. There were trips to the Rose Bowl, Las Vegas and San Francisco, and my kids loved going to the games that I did in Iowa City and Des Moines. I took Diane with me when I covered the premier of "All the President's Men" at Hancher Auditorium in Iowa City. She met Robert Redford in person.

Jane and Diane were complete opposites growing up. Both had bubbly personalities, but Jane was a straight A student at Hoover High; she was in all the school plays and was a class officer. She was on Younkers Teen Board.

Daughter Jane

Then it was off to Iowa State (yes, she took a fair amount of razzing at the time, but Iowa State had the courses she wanted). She continued her excellent study habits and graduated 8th out of a class of one thousand in Industrial Administration (that was at a time when women were starting to be hired in management positions at manufacturing and financial institutions.) She also served as vice-president of the Pi Phi sorority. Jane did her best to help me in my relationship with the Cyclone fans. That's when I was also doing Iowa State basketball games. Our official WHO banner, which we displayed at every game, was done in Iowa's colors, old gold and black. Jane, who was an excellent seamstress, made one for me in Iowa State colors, cardinal and gold. It didn't help. I still got the finger from a few Cyclone fans, and one group of students held up a sign that read, "WHO hires the handicapped".

With Jane

Jane is still active in school and civic affairs in the Davenport area. She is married to Jeff Paul, a partner in the Lane and Waterman law firm. They have three children, Annie (married to Brian Gibson), A.J. and Charlie, and I am proud to say, I have my first great grandchild, Christopher Paul Gibson.

Jane and her husband, Jeff Paul

My grandchildren: AJ, Annie, and Charlie

My great-grandson, Christopher Gibson

Daughter Diane

Diane was an incubator baby, but as I told her later, she made up for it the rest of her life. She was a genuine free spirit. Many people told me she was the "cutest kid in her class". She loved gymnastics (we had a trampoline in our backyard), but readin', writin' and Shakespeare were not her style. She grew up too fast. I once said that between Byron Rice grade school and Meredith Junior High, she changed from Shirley Temple to Marilyn Monroe. I empathized with her. She had the same kind of high-spirited personality that I had as a kid, but I told her if you don't get an education, it's a dead end street. It was a tough time for her. Her mother suffered from chronic ill health for several years and then developed cancer. Mary Jan passed away in November of 1985.

I plunged harder than ever into my work and added the Iowa Barnstormers to my broadcasting schedule. I also traveled to Korea and China with the Iowa basketball team, then later on to London, Paris and Amsterdam. Diane, by that time, had moved to Pasadena, California and had married a childhood boyfriend, Bill Webster.

Wedding Day for daughter, Diane

The biggest change in my own life came on a trip to the condo I owned in Scottsdale, Arizona. I invited Randy and Paula Duncan over before going out to dinner. They were visiting friends in the area. Earlier that day, I had met a young lady by the pool, who lived there. Her name was Jill Williams, and she was from San Francisco. She was, I thought, a knockout.

Trying to impress her, I played a recording of a football game that I had done. She said, "That's fine, but what do you do for a living?" Randy got a big kick out of that. So we all went out to dinner, and that's where it all started.

Despite busy schedules and distance, Jill and I went together steadily, doing a lot of traveling and going to football games and basketball tournaments. I surprised Jill with the announcement of our wedding date at a marvelous party given at Glen Oaks Country Club by Bill Krause and Gary Kirke. Jill and I were married on April 12, 1997, in Scottsdale, at the beautiful home of Carol and Wayne Carpenter.

Jill and daughter Jenni

Jill, Jeff (son), Jenni (daughter), and Jim

Jill has two children, Jenni and Jeff, both in their early 30s and now full-fledged members of our enlarged family. Both are enjoying successful careers. Jenni is a Montessori teacher and Head of School in Irvine, California. Jeff is a gourmet chef in Scottsdale. He has prepared many delicious meals for us.

I have always been an optimist—it's my trademark, I guess. I think I inherited it from my father. He once told me he survived the Depression because he never allowed himself to become depressed. I am the same way. Now, I will admit, I have never been happier. Jill is my soulmate, my best friend, my alter-ego, my sweetheart, my medical supervisor

My exercise for the day: bouncing on the backyard trampoline

Photo printed with permission by the Des Moines Register

(as required) and a gourmet cook as well. I'll be honest, I would not be here today without her nursing and making sure I have a proper diet. And, she has a sense of humor to match mine.

I told her when I reach 90 (which is not too far away) I am going to drink a martini, smoke a cigar, and wink at the girls. Jill said, "And if you can get a date, I'll drive you."

Actually, the spring of 2009 had been tough on me. I got pneumonia, among other ills, and then I received shocking news from Pasadena. My daughter, Diane, who had been sick for some time with serious internal problems, had passed away at the age of 48. I was devastated. She and I were very close. She called me every week.

I remember her final call. It touched my heart as I thought of it, and the tears filled my eyes.

She said, "Dad, you remember all those things you told me when I was 16? You were right. I'll always be your little girl and do everything you want me to."

I only wish I could go back again to that little girl in the park.

AFTERWORD

Sixty-five years ago, if someone had asked me to write a fictional account of the games, events and people I would cover in my career, I could not have possibly come up with anything to match the reality as it occurred.

When I walked into WHO on May 17, 1944, I never dreamed in my wildest fantasies that I would have the opportunity to be part of so much drama, excitement and history. Looking back over the more than 6,000 play-by-play events that I have covered, it astounds me to realize how many thousands of fans share those same memories with me—because I have been there for all the upset victories and last-second finishes that have thrilled Hawkeye fans for more than six decades...from Nile Kinnick to Randy Duncan to Chuck Long to Ricky Stanzi, from Evy to Hayden to Kirk, from the "Fabulous Five" to Freddie Brown to Ronnie Lester, from Ralph Miller to Lute to Tom Davis, and more. Plus all the other personalities I knew and worked with, and the hundreds of memorable experiences that were a part of my life and times on WHO and WHO-TV. It's all in here, and I have loved it...loved it...loved it!!!

Jim Zabel

TO BE CONTINUED!

We hope you have enjoyed *Jim Zabel—65 Years of Fun and Games*. A second Jim Zabel book will be coming next year, where Jim tells behind-the-scenes storires about University of Iowa football and basketball players. If you have an interesting Jim Zabel story, please email it to us for possible inclusion in this book. Email it to printedpage@cox.net (please put JIM ZABEL in the subject line and be sure to include a phone number where you can be reached), or call the author directly at (602) 738-5889.

OTHER BOOKS BY RICH WOLFE

Remembering Harry Kalas
Da Coach (Mike Ditka)
I Remember Harry Caray
There's No Expiration Date on Dreams (Tom Brady)
He Graduated Life with Honors and No Regrets (Pat Tillman)
Take This Job and Love It (Jon Gruden)
Been There, Shoulda Done That (John Daly)
Oh, What a Knight (Bob Knight)
And the Last Shall Be First (Kurt Warner)
Remembering Jack Buck
Sports Fans Who Made Headlines
Fandemonium
Remembering Dale Earnhardt
I Saw It On the Radio (Vin Scully)
Tim Russert, We Heartily Knew Ye
The Real McCoy (Al McCoy, Phoenix Suns announcer)
Personal Foul (With Tim Donaghy, former NBA referee)

For Yankee Fans Only
For Cubs Fans Only
For Red Sox Fans Only
For Cardinals Fans Only
For Packers Fans Only
For Hawkeye Fans Only
For Browns Fans Only
For Mets Fans Only
For Notre Dame Fans Only—
   The New Saturday Bible
For Bronco Fans Only
For Nebraska Fans Only

For Buckeye Fans Only
For Georgia Bulldog Fans Only
For South Carolina Fans Only
For Clemson Fans Only
For Cubs Fans Only—Volume II
For Oklahoma Fans Only
For Yankee Fans Only—Volume II
For Mizzou Fans Only
For Kansas City Chiefs Fans Only
For K-State Fans Only
For KU Fans Only (Kansas)
For Phillies Fans Only

Next book to be released:
A Perfect 10 (with Ron Santos of the Chicago Cubs)

All books are the same size, format and price.
Questions? Contact the author directly at 602-738-5889.